DEEP SO

D E E P
SOCIALISM

**A New Manifesto
of
Marxist Ethics and Economics**

Peter Wilberg

New Gnosis Publications, London

First published by New Gnosis Publications
www.newgnosis.co.uk

Printed and bound in England by Antony Rowe Ltd
Distributed by Gardners Books, Eastbourne, Sussex

ISBN 1-904519-02-4

Capitalist freedom and individualism is a spurious freedom and individualism – the freedom of the consumer to spend money only earned through compulsory wage-slavery. Real communism is *authentic individualism* – a society in which, as Marx himself defined it "the free development of *each* is the condition for the free development of *all.*"

CONTENTS

PREFACE

Deep Socialism is a Marxian socialist manifesto for the twenty-first century. It is based on a new dialectical theory of value, one which not only reaffirms and reapplies the analysis of economic value presented in Das Kapital, but complements and integrates it with an analysis of ethical, ecological and educational value exploitation in capitalist society. Deep Socialism is radical socialism, not only because it digs down to the hidden roots of the market economic system, but because it exposes the false conflict between economism and moralism, the ideology of "shareholder value" promoted by investment fund managers and the clerical advocacy of traditional "shared values".

The dialectical theory of value articulated in this manifesto is the product of over thirty years' reflection on issues of socialist ethics and economics, which began when I first read the Communist Manifesto of Marx and Engels. This was before the onslaught of Thatcherism and Reaganism, before the demise of the Soviet Union and the end of the Cold War. Today, as right wing commentators bask in the "defeat" of socialism and reaffirm the original principles of unfettered market economics, it is high time that socialists once again challenge these principles, not only ethically but economically. Yet to talk about socialist ethics "and" economics misses the point. The "labour theory of value" developed by Marx in Das Kapital, his analysis of how "surplus value" is extracted from labour in the form of profit and rent, was intrinsically interwoven with a fundamental socialist ethic. This ethic was based on the understanding that each person's labour has the same worth as every other's, and went together with the vision of a communist society in which work, instead of being a means to an end, would be an intrinsic source of deep value fulfilment.

The fact that the same term – "value" – can be used to refer to the "use value" of things, to the economic value of commodities and of labour as a commodity, and to personal and social "values" is not a linguistic accident but an expression of a profound inner relation between ethics and economics that not even Marx explored in all its depths and ramifications. Dialectical value theory reaffirms and redevelops Marx's theory of value so as to bring out more clearly the dialectical relation *between* ethical and economic value(s), and in this way to shed new light on the most important ethical and economic issues of our day. It takes basic economic key words such as "value", "cost", "time", "employment" and "profit" and explores their deep social and ethical dimensions as well as their surface economic ones. Its aim is to expose the fundamental misunderstanding of the relation between economic and ethical value(s) that lies at the heart of capitalist ideology. The misguided "ethics" of the church and its efforts to promote "moral education", and the misguided economics of left-liberal advocates of the "social market" are both an expression of this ideology. And yet the fundamental mis-relation of ethical and economic concepts in capitalist thinking expresses a fundamental mis-relation of ethics and economics in capitalist society. It is not just a theoretical mis-relation but a real one affecting millions of people. Understanding and overcoming this mis-relation is not just a theoretical task but a practical one.

Dialectical value distinguishes itself from any purely economic or ethical, material or spiritual, psychological or biological view of human values. It is based on a fundamental distinction between symbolic values which are expressed in languages and currencies, communicative and commercial exchange, and deep values, embodied in the individual qualities that people bring to their work and relationships, and through which they imbue them with value. The Dialectics of Value(s) has broad practical implications which cannot be restricted to the specialist domains of ethical and economic theory, for it also transforms our personal and social-scientific understanding of health and education, psychology and politics, religion and culture.

The first part of this manifesto presents a new critique not just of the ethics and economics of the market but of its culture – the culture of marketing – one which transforms all deep human values and cultural symbols into commodities. I use the concepts of negative value and negative surplus value, negative time and negative quality, to show its effects on the environment, health and education. In doing so I offer a new "deep socialist perspective": counter-posing deep health to superficial symbolic health, deep education to abstract symbolic education, deep profit to symbolic financial profit and deep politics to the moral marketing of political personalities and policies.

The second part of the manifesto moves from the Dialectics of Value(s) to the Ethics of Dialogue – extending Marx's analysis of value from the sphere of economic relations, commerce and commodity exchange to the sphere of human relations, culture and communicative exchange. Its aim is to show that the true link between economics and politics on the one hand, and culture and education on the other, is not "moral education" or "emotional education" but the intrinsic connection between *valuing* and *learning*. It introduces the principles and praxis of "relational learning" – learning to value others and valuing what we learn from others. Herein, values are defined as individual human qualities embodied in relating to others and materialised in labour. This understanding of values as embodied relational qualities is counter-posed to economic, political and psychoanalytic theories which interpret and value these qualities only symbolically, through their expression in cultural symbols and symbolic behaviour, communication and commerce, spoken languages and traded words and traded currencies.

In the third part of this manifesto, I set out new principles for socialist political education, organisation and leadership, based on the praxis of relational learning and relational thinking – of Dialogical Ethics and Dialectical Thinking. Their basis is the understanding that the socialist transformation of economic relations can only come about through a transformation of the human relations on which the market economy is based and which it reproduces. Human beings need to relate to others in society, not principally in order to be valued for the individual qualities they embody, but precisely in order to embody those individual qualities – to embody them *in* their relating. Deep Socialism is fulfilled individualism – a social individualism in which deep relational value fulfilment replaces the purely symbolic value fulfilment of atomised individuals and groups in the market economy.

Part 1

From Equality to Quality of Life

Beyond the Ethics and Economics of the Market

Cherish the old to understand the new.
Japanese proverb

A New Communist Manifesto?

The Communist Manifesto of 1848 opened with the famous words "A spectre is haunting Europe: the spectre of communism." With the collapse of Soviet-style "communism" many believed Marxism to be dead and this spectre to be finally exorcised. In fact, the last decades of the twentieth century saw Marx's theory of capitalist development confirmed in every respect. As quoted in the British newspaper The Independent, Douglas McWilliams, the former chief economic adviser to the Confederation of British Industry, describes the out performance of the US economy as a result of a "transformation in the operation of capitalism on a sufficient scale to justify being described as a reinvention....Real pay is rising a lot less fast than productivity, and the surplus is being handed over to profits. If that is seen to work in US financial markets, there will be pressure to extend it to Europe. and to the UK in particular." It is therefore high time to "reinvent" deep Marxist socialism, and to fight against a capitalist system which "rewards fund managers with tens or even hundred of millions of dollars in share options while holding down ordinary workers' pay." (Magnus Grimond, The Independent 28.4.97).

The phenomenon of "globalisation" fully bears out Marx's understanding that only with the establishment of a totally globalised corporate market economy would the inherent contradictions of capitalism come to a head – the creation of a huge "reserve army" of unemployed, the exacerbation of disparities between rich and poor, the elimination of the "middle class" and the tendency to a Brazilian style 20/80 division of the world – an upper twenty percent of the population with jobs and relatively high incomes, sitting on top of a huge global "underclass" including the under-nourished, under-paid, under-employed and unemployed. The "spectre of communism" haunts the global economy in another way too. For in order to cut costs and maintain their competitiveness, global corporations find themselves driven in the direction of increased *cooperation* with suppliers, customers and even competitors. Hence the fetish made of pseudo-ethical "value statements" and pseudo-socialist principles of empowerment and teamwork in order to raise quality, productivity and morale. And yet the immense value placed on "service" symbolises also the contrary emergence of neo-feudal relations between companies higher up on the supply chain and those beneath them. The mystical maxim "As above, so below" is ruthlessly enforced as Original Equipment Manufacturers impose ever-tighter quality, cost and delivery conditions on their suppliers, who in turn pass them on to sub-suppliers further down the chain. "Downsizing" and "rationalisation" continue in the drive to boost shareholder value, intensifying the exploitation of those still in work. The deep values of a company lie, as managers symbolically concede, in its employees and the individual human qualities they embody in their work and relationships. This means, however, that they are not the private property of individuals nor of shareholders. They cannot be bought like parts or branded like commodities. But who dares raise a communist challenge to the market economy, capitalist property relations and the value exploitation of labour today?

The economic and ethical foundations of socialist theory and praxis are under attack as never before. This attack comes from three main sources: from the TINA principle – the belief that There Is No Alternative to the market economy, a belief to which both social democrats and left-leaning intellectuals have bowed; from clerical and social moralists of both left and right, who speak of "traditional values", "family values" or "community values" in abstraction from concrete social and economic relations, and real human relationships; and from a third source – the pseudo-religious pursuers of the "eternal gene", who think that all human social attributes and behaviour can be reduced to biology and offer salvation through technologies of gene manipulation.

The economic attack on socialism overlooks the fact that modern information technology now makes possible a devolved, efficient and ecologically balanced planned economy free of the sort of bureaucratic waste, inefficiency and privilege associated with the now defunct Soviet economies. Their problems were partly due to the massive and long-term diversion of resources into military-industrial production, and partly also to a plain lack of computing power. As Cockshott and Cottrel report in their book "Towards a New Socialism", in the 1980's it was argued that the sheer number of calculations required to produce an integrated economic plan for a single region such as the Ukraine would take the whole of the world's population ten million years.

Existing mainframe computers were inadequate for the task, in contrast to those of today – which could as easily be applied to the creation of an information network for macro-economic planning as to the creation of information systems for business corporations and the stock exchange. In the meantime, erstwhile defenders of the German "social market economy" and proponents of a new model "stake holder economy", on the other hand, find themselves impotent in the face of the ever-intensifying pressures of international, and particularly American finance capitalism, to boost their dividends and return on capital. It is an extraordinary paradox to see leading German conservative politicians such as the prime minister of Bavaria rail passionately against "shareholder value" and short-term financial profit-making in their addresses to corporate managers and bosses. Yet this passion is a clear expression of the irresolvable contradiction they are now caught in – between the values and principles of the social market on the one hand – social partnership with the unions and a generous welfare state – and the new realities of global capitalism on the other.

There is now no way back to the social market that post-war political conditions made possible for a while in West Germany – a form of capitalism which US fund managers regarded as a neo-socialist aberration, giving them a poor return on capital. There is only one way forward – to a fully socialist economy. For with the increasing pressure from trans-national financial markets to increase return on capital in the name of "shareholder value", corporate managers find themselves forced to abandon any notions of deep cost or social responsibility and to sacrifice even profitable production sites to achieve higher share prices or dividends. If they are not bought off themselves by share option schemes and bonuses, or reduced to acquiescence by their own job insecurity, managers are left to operate in an ethical vacuum, lacking any broader economic, social or political perspective by which to question and challenge prevailing jargons and ideologies. When these same ideologies are echoed by social democrats and left-wing intellectuals, as well as by bankers, fund managers and CEOs it is no wonder that managers do not challenge them themselves.

For the unions the question is simple. Only by global cooperation and organisation – a new Workers Internationale – can they resist the effects of global deregulation and make it less easy for corporations to play off workers in England or Germany against each other or against those in Mexico or Poland. But for both managers and workers the essential question is not "What can we do?" but what "What can I do?". Workers must decide individually whether it is worth their while to join a union, and fight to protect their rights. Managers must decide individually whether they are prepared to take account of deeper issues and deeper costs in their decisions. The challenge is both an ethical and an intellectual one. For unless the current ideologies are challenged intellectually, those managers, clerics and intellectuals who speak from their heart and conscience will be regarded as well-meaning wimps, soft on the unions, or with some truth, as unable to face the "realities" of the market economy.

The fetishism of moral phraseology expressed in terms such as "family values", "traditional values", "community values" etc. makes the fundamental mistake of treating values as the *private property* of individuals or groups, ignoring the fact that the only values that can be "held" as property or exchanged for other values are money, property, stocks or shares. Values are not the property of individuals, families, social or ethnic groups, political parties or nations – they are the real human qualities that people discover and embody in their relationships with *other* individuals, families, groups and cultures. Moral education cannot substitute for what I call "relational learning". This means learning to value the human qualities embodied by others and valuing what we can learn from them. But the individual qualities that others embody in their way of relating are not the product of their symbolic values – their cultural symbols or symbolic behaviour. Nor can they be reduced to a set of generic moral concepts or beliefs. To speak of "family" or "community" values in a generic way is tantamount to devaluing the specific moral qualities embodied by each particular family or community, in its specificity and uniqueness.

The third attack on socialism is more concealed and sinister in its implications, for the worship of race that produced the

Holocaust is no more perverse than the worship of the gene; pseudo-religious genetics being no less perverse than pseudo-scientific "eugenics". If crime and violence are seen, not as by-products of the market economy, but as genetically determined behaviours, then all that is required to control them is genetic screening and manipulation. That both nature and nurture, race and culture, biology and sociology, play a role in shaping behaviour and "moral character" is indisputable. But so do *beliefs* about genes and beliefs about "values". Today, genetics has become a new scientific religion with its own neo-Darwinian world-view and ethics – another way of translating what goes on *between* people into something going on *in* them. The geneticists' attacks on the socialist critique of the market, nevertheless, hold important keys for the new understanding of socialist ethics and economics. For it is only by analysing the dialectical relation between genetic and environmental, biological and cultural, ethical and economic aspects of individual behaviour that eugenic "solutions" can be challenged.

Genes are not the "determinants" of human behaviour. Even to talk about "criminal genes" or a "gene for schizophrenia" (let alone to try and prove their existence) is to conflate a form of socially construed behaviour – "criminality" or "schizophrenia" – with a deep genetic disposition, as if this symbolic behaviour were the only form in which the genetic disposition could express itself. The conflation of symbolic behaviours and genetic disposition in science parallels the conflation of symbolic and deep values in religious ethics. No matter how many studies are conducted which appear to "prove" the genetic basis of mental illness, crime or intelligence, all fall prey to this category confusion. The worst examples of such studies are those that attempt to "prove" that "intelligence" is racially determined. The opponents of such studies miss the point entirely, reducing it to a matter of statistics or "political correctness". But one does not need to dispute any scientific evidence or wave a pink flag to see that what is really questionable is not the statistics or the politics of the researchers but the very definition of "intelligence" on which their studies are based. The idea that a person's intelligence can be reduced to the particular type of mental gymnastics required to do an "IQ" test is no less absurd than believing one could gauge someone's moral character and maturity by giving them a test on the Bible.

As we pass the 150th anniversary of the publication of the Communist Manifesto, the attacks on socialism are wearing ever thinner. And if we cast our minds forward to 150 years hence, it seems even more unlikely than ever that the market economy will survive. It is far more likely to be regarded in retrospect itself as a temporary and chaotic phase of social-economic development, one which rapidly accelerated the very processes of technological and social changes that will make its gradual demise inevitable. For the global conflicts, inequalities and environmental dangers that these changes have thrown up, now pose, as Marx long ago predicted they would, insuperable challenges to the basic principles of the "free market". They reveal the true nature of this freedom as an unrestricted and deregulated freedom to devalue and exploit our social, cultural and natural environment on a global scale. But the transition to a non-market economy will not come about through a Leninist-style political seizure of state power by the working masses. Nor will it come about by social democratic tinkering with the market and the attempt to soften its hard edges. Instead the seeds of socialism will thrive on the very chaos and diversity of the contemporary world, through a grass-roots change in the human and economic relations on which the market economy is based. Not only new forms of cooperative enterprise and partnership but new forms of trade and economic cooperation between hitherto competing corporations and nations will grow up, redefining the strategic goals of business life and embodying new values. For, the more passionately and desperately corporations seek measures to raise their competitiveness, the more they reveal a deep crisis in the ethic and rationality of competition itself, in the ethics and economics of the market.

Economic and Ethical Value Exploitation

The basis of socialist economics lies in Marx's distinction between the use-value of a commodity – its value in satisfying a human need – and its exchange value, expressed in money. The basis of socialist ethics lies in a fundamental distinction between the real human qualities *embodied* by individuals in their relationships and materialised in their work, and the way these qualities are symbolised in their language, culture and behaviour. Individual human qualities can be compared to "moral genes".

The symbolic behaviours and cultural symbols through which these qualities are expressed are no more *determined* by our biological genes, than is the exchange value of a commodity determined by the real human qualities that go into its production and imbue it with value. Marx showed that in a market economy, the material attributes and qualities that give commodities their use value become merely the symbolic expression of their exchange value. But monetary exchange value is itself one form of symbolic value. Symbolic value is also shaped by the cultural symbols attached to commodities through advertising and marketing. Today's global market economy is dominated by the ubiquitous culture and symbolism of the market itself – the culture of marketing and the symbolism of advertising. This culture is the antithesis of all culture, "creatively" transforming all cultural symbols into marketing tools, and the deep values they express into commodities. Today, no ethnic, ethical, cultural or spiritual symbols are sacrosanct in the hands of "creative" agencies who with them seek to transform commodities themselves into the symbolic materialisation of every conceivable value from freedom to femininity, faith to fatherhood. Symbolic value consumption and spiritual consumerism replace the embodiment and fulfilment of deep values. The culture of marketing is therefore the fourth, most obvious but also most insidious, attack on the human foundations of an ethical socialist economy. For it is not only an ideology but an economic reality.

The true source of economic value is not the exchange process but human labour time and the qualities that human beings embody in their labour and materialise in its products. The true source of cultural values is not symbols or symbolic commodities but the deep values embodied in these human qualities themselves. But in capitalist society, labour is itself a commodity. Its value is reduced to the market price of human labour power. Labour time is measured and remunerated only quantitatively, devaluing the qualities which employees bring to their work and rewarding its resulting quality, if at all, only in the form of bonuses. Pay differentials are based principally on type of work rather than quality, on what people do rather than how well they do it. But why should a slap dash lawyer earn many times more per hour than a caring nurse or teacher? Why should a poor quality manager earn more than a hard-working assembly line worker who thinks up time-saving procedures? Such inequalities are neither necessary economic "facts of life", nor merely ethically regrettable inequalities. In negating the equal worth of all human labour, whatever its type, they devalue the particular qualities that each worker brings to his work.

Values are individual qualities that are valued – qualities such as creativity, dedication, care, honesty, attention to detail etc. But if earnings are based principally on the symbolic, market value attached to particular types of work, these qualities are essentially devalued, whatever "bonus" systems are introduced to acknowledge them. Symbolic values replace the deep values that individuals bring to and seek to fulfil through their work. In this way the market economy transforms human labour and the qualities it embodies into a means to an end rather than an end in itself, into a competitive struggle for symbolic value recognition, remuneration and fulfilment, and symbolic value consumption.

Because individuals in a market economy find their own labour devalued and exploited for profit they may seek value fulfilment in recreation and relationships. But the circle is then complete, for through the culture of marketing the market economy can once more derive economic profit from the conversion of deep values into symbolic ones – by selling back to workers the very human qualities which it devalued in the labour process, but this time, symbolically, as commodities. The chief competition for the cultural value symbols offered by institutionalised religion, therefore, comes not from occult sects or a changing sexual culture, nor from cultural pluralism or individualism but from the commodification of values itself, from the culture of marketing and spiritual consumerism. It makes no difference here whether the product is a burger, a bra, or a religious belief system. The culture of marketing transforms the deepest values into imaginary attributes of commodities, and commodities into imaginary embodiments of whatever cultural symbols it finds marketable. Not only this, in the culture of marketing, individuals must market themselves – tailoring their own deep values to suit the current symbols which determine which human qualities are valued and which not. All individuals and groups who seek to restore or renew traditional values, or to affirm new ones, must, in order to reach their audience, first bow down to the demands of the market place and become consumers of symbolic values – must devalue the very values they seek to promote by marketing them as symbols and commodities. The growth of cultural diversity, the proliferation of alternative life-styles, religions, world outlooks and therapies in our "post-modern" world poses no essential challenge to the capitalist value system so long as their advocates heed the call of the market and reduce the deep values they seek to embody to symbolic ones acceptable to the modern-day spiritual consumer.

Marx saw the way in which religions and idealist philosophies exalted immaterial or "spiritual" values above material ones as the ghostly ideological reflection of a real social process: the process by which capitalism transformed material products and living human labour into physical expressions of something equally mysterious and immaterial – their exchange value on the market. Modern marketing seeks to make spiritual values once again manifest in matter – not in the use value of commodities, but in toothpaste or cars. Capitalism cannot boast of a culture, which acknowledges the equal spiritual worth of each individual whilst denying the equal value of different types of labour. Managers cannot make a fetish of quality whilst undervaluing or overvaluing the human qualities embodied in different types of work. Societies cannot boast of spiritual values, whilst marketing them as commodities. Nor can clerical moralists speak of how much deep spiritual values *matter* whilst denying the values that the human spirit materialises in human labour. It is the undervaluation and overvaluation of different types of work, irrespective of quality, and not any lack of moral education or indoctrination, that leads to the progressive *demoralisation* of individuals and society.

Nowadays, not only "new" social democrats but the traditional churches and religions too, are prone to worry whether they are "marketing" themselves well enough. Yet the culture of marketing has its roots in the translation of deep values into symbolic "religious" ones. Each religion seeks not only to represent and communicate certain deep values through its own symbols, but to identify these values *with* its particular symbols – thereby allowing it to claim a monopoly on them. To the extent that they succeed, however, they also remove their claim to be the ethical voice of society, for in the process they undo the fundamental ethical distinction between deep values and symbolic ones, sacrificing the latter to the former as the market economy and culture of marketing now does to perfection. All religions claim "truth" for their symbols, their rituals, icons and holy scriptures; validly so, in so far as these symbols have their source in deep values. Validly also in so far as they help individuals to genuinely embody them as human relational qualities and not just espouse or express them symbolically. But invalidly in so far as these deep values are identified with, or reduced to, symbolic ones. The profane economic culture of marketing, and the sacrilegious symbolism of advertising, are matched in its obscene symbolic obsessions only by the fanaticism with which dismayed religious fundamentalists seek to reassert their own monopoly over ethics and deep values.

Whereas in Russia and Eastern Europe the ethics and economics of the market have clearly created a monetary, material and moral-spiritual morass, it appears at first sight self-evident that capitalism has succeeded in rapidly raising living standards for large numbers of people in both the Asia-Pacific countries and in China. This has been achieved, however, through pursuing a model of economic growth aimed at matching the unsustainable patterns of consumption, waste and environmental depletion followed by the West. In China, as in the West, "standard of living" is identified not primarily with the satisfaction of material or spiritual needs, but with symbolic consumption and the accumulation of symbolic capital – earning enough to drink Coca Cola, to buy expensive, usually foreign, brand names, or to send one's children to elite private schools. Education or extra-curricular tuition, once free, now demands massive investment of earnings. Whereas in the past workers found little to buy in the state-run shop, now they spend their hard-earned money paying over-the-top prices for "premium", high-status branded products – whether imported from the West or manufactured by low-wage workers in their own country who gain nothing from the symbolic inflation of their products. Whereas in the past all that was available were shoddy goods from state-run factories, now "quality" and "quality of life" are associated merely with expensive brands and keeping up with consumer fashions. Along with the principle of "to he who has, shall be given" is added "he who has now a bit more, shall pay for his symbols".

From Equality of Labour to Quality of Work

The chosen representatives of both God and Mammon, church and capitalism, always seek to identify deep human values with their spiritual or material symbols, old or new. Socialist ethics and economics are not the ethics of mullahs or the economics of marketing men. And yet a leap forward for society beyond the market economy requires an ethical leap of faith as well as a leap in understanding. For, the leap of understanding represented by both the economic and ethical dialectics of value is a return to the ethic-economic origin of socialism – the preparedness to take a moral stand on the fundamental *equality* of all forms of labour, not irrespective of their *quality* but irrespective of the symbolic value the market gives to the human qualities they embody.

To whom does a manager owe his deepest loyalty – to corporate objectives or mission statements, to shareholders and fund managers, or to the company's employees as a whole? To whom does a union leader owe his deepest loyalty? To the workers in "his" shop or plant, to workers in the company as a whole – including its foreign plants, shops and offices? Such questions are important not only for individuals. All important business decisions ultimately hinge on them. Every section of a company, as of society as a whole, has its own implicit ranking of objectives and values according to its own needs and interests. When it comes to deciding between alternative strategies and courses of action, each of these value rankings can be presented as a rational one – albeit on the implicit basis of that ranking. The idea that there is some higher order rationale for decision making that is itself value free is untenable. Only when we understand that all reasons for a particular course of action are ultimately *rationalisations* of a particular type of deep or symbolic value ranking can the parameters of business costing and decision-making be properly broadened and deepened.

A purely ethical critique of capitalist "greed" for profit cannot change the world. Just as right-wing theorists have turned to the original doctrines of free market economics in order to justify the competitive pursuit of profit at any cost, so must socialist theory return to the basic principles of socialist economics. These offer far more radical solutions to current world problems than either free-market economics or the social-democratic illusion of a "social market". At the heart of socialist economics is the belief that a social *democracy* is meaningless without an *economic* democracy. Today, what we call "democracy" is soured by the fact that in practice only those with the money, connections and resources necessary to finance political campaigns have any chance of winning elections. What we call democracy is a state in which all have the right to express their own opinions – but few the wealth to promulgate them. In which The Many have the right to speak freely but The Few do not feel called upon to listen – except in order to translate what they hear into their own terms and twist it to their purposes.

Deep Socialism is democratic socialism, based on the principles of social democracy and economic socialism. Democracy is based on the principle that each person's vote carries equal weight, irrespective of their wealth or status: On equality of rights. Socialist economics is based on the principle that each person's labour has the same basic value as every other person's, irrespective of its nature: On equality of labour. Why should a corporate boss earn hundreds more per hour than a hard-working secretary, cleaner or assembly-line worker? Apologists for capitalism claim that only in this way are incentives provided for people to work harder, and to gain more knowledge and skills of the sort that society needs. But since when have teachers earned big bucks for working harder, improving their skills, and doing a better job? Only an economy in which people are paid on an equal basis according to their labour time can be called socialist. In such an economy the value of specialist skills would *already* have been paid for through the free education and training that was provided to them. Hourly pay differentials would be based not on what people did, but on how they did it. Not on the nature of their work but on its quality. As it is, individuals in a capitalist, market economy are frequently forced to choose between value-fulfilling work that is economically under-valued and under-paid, value-negating work that is economically over-valued and overpaid, or, as is most common, value-adding work that gives more than it gets. In a socialist economy, all workers would be paid the same basic hourly rate – not in money but in "smart card" entitlements to whatever products and services they choose to obtain. Systems of earning differentials would be based solely on distinctions in the quality of the time and work that individuals put in. These quality differentials would be decided democratically. Individuals who preferred to work at the minimum quality level established by a collective would be under no pressure to raise their productivity – they would simply get the basic rate.

The ethical principle of equal pay for equal hours, whatever one's work or position, would allow quality to become the principal basis of pay differentials. But quality of labour depends on the quality of the time people give to their work, and time quality cannot be measured in the same way as time quantity. Innovations require thinking time and incubation time – deep quality time. This deep time is also broad time, for quality and creative innovation are often the expression of many years of experience, or of many weeks and months of thought. That is why, in a socialist economy, quality differentials can only be determined cooperatively and democratically by employees through mutual evaluation of the quality of each other's labour and of its products. Mutual quality evaluation does not discriminate between the human qualities and skills required by different types of work. It discriminates only the quantitative degree to which each individual actually invests their skills and qualities in their work – the quality of the time they give it. It does not give work different quantitative hourly rates. It merely adds a qualitative dimension to the measurement of labour time. A socialist economy thereby grants full value to the skills and qualities of each worker, not according to the nature of these skills and qualities but according to the extent to which they are applied, embodied and materialised.

The establishment of a democratic, planned economy and the phasing out of money in favour of labour time-and-quality credits recorded on smart cards would take advantage of the enormous developments in information and communications technology brought about by computers and microchips. In this way the basic Marxist theory of social development and transformation would be fulfilled: namely that it is development in the technology of production that makes changes in the economic structure of society both necessary and *possible*. Information technology would render unnecessary the bureaucratic waste and privilege associated with the planned economies of the erstwhile Soviet Union and its satellites, together with the inequalities these economies maintained. The disasters of previous "socialisms" pale in comparison with the social, economic, and ethical morass being created by today's global market economy. To bring about a democratic, money-less, computer-planned economy based on equality of different types of labour requires, first of all, that individuals have the moral and intellectual courage to reject TINA – the idea that There Is No Alternative to the global market economy, and that the best that can be done is to ameliorate its effects through a "social market". The redistribution of wealth in a non-market, deep socialist economy would ensure not only that the basic needs of all the world's people are met, but that each receives according to their work and not according to their social status. What would diminish is only the consumption of hollow symbolic values created by the culture of marketing. Redistribution would raise both average quantity and average quality of personal consumption to a level higher than the market can provide on a global basis.

The ethics of the market economy lie in a model of inter-human relationships in which each individual freely *competes* with each other for value fulfilment and for symbolic recognition of their "own" needs and qualities. Price differentials and pay inequalities based on market valuations of different types of commodity, including labour, reflect the tendency of individuals to maintain their self-worth by either undervaluing or overvaluing those qualities in others that they devalue in themselves – qualities that are similar and yet different. The deep values that link people in families, ethnic and cultural groups are not private property because they are based not on similarities or differences but similarities-in-difference – in "simference". The model of human relations on which socialism is based is a cooperative one, based on acknowledging that it is precisely in those ways in which other individuals and groups appear most different to us that our deepest value kinships become symbolically manifest. Alongside the equal value given to different types of labour in a deep socialist economy, and the consequent redistribution of wealth, would be an equal recognition of the deep values expressed in different cultures and cultural identities. But just as the abolition of pay differentials would not abolish quality differentials, so would the abolition of cultural discrimination not abolish cultural differences. And yet individual cultural identity would not need to be guarded and protected in the way it is now – simply by clinging onto the shared *symbols* of a culture, or forcing them down the throats of others. For, each individual only truly fulfils their cultural identity and its deep values by *embodying* this identity and these values in their relationships to other individuals and cultures – not by holding on to a set of symbols or rituals. Deep socialism would therefore promote neither a totalitarian Mono-culture exalting Sameness nor a Multi-culture exalting Difference. Instead it would allow a creative *Trans-culture* to emerge – a culture in which identity is understood as relational identity – and not as private property. In which *new* symbols would emerge from the simference, synergy and creative interaction of individual cultural identities and values.

Quality, Time and Value

"Growth" in a capitalist economy means quantitative economic growth only, "profit" merely economic profit. The pursuit of profit for profit's sake and growth for growth's sake is a purely quantitative and symbolic expression of the natural human striving for maximum, *qualitative* value fulfilment – deep value fulfilment. Only a socialist economy can create a society in which the rationally planned satisfaction of material needs is not the condition but the result of satisfying this basic spiritual need. In which "the free development of each is the condition for the free development of all. *The Communist Manifesto*

Labour is the embodiment of individual qualities in working relationships and their materialisation in production. It is the source of symbolic, economic value because it imbues products and services with the deep values linking individuals and embodied in their relational qualities – the way they relate to each other and their work. The *intrinsic value* of a product or service derives from these qualities and is something qualitative. The quality of products and services, on the other hand, is, paradoxically, something quantitative. It depends on the degree to which these qualities are embodied and materialised in the labour process. But the market value of a product or service depends on the symbolic value attached to these qualities, and not merely on their intrinsic value or their use value to the consumer.

Use value in a market economy is *symbolic* use and value, as well as material use and consumption. In a market economy, therefore, work imbues products and services with intrinsic qualities and deep values but is valued only symbolically. The symbolic value of different types of labour is expressed through their "market value". Because different types of work have a different symbolic value in the capitalist system they are paid differently according to their "market value". But pay differentials, which are determined principally by the symbolic, market value of different *types* of labour is payment that devalues *quality* of labour, usually with the consequence that it is under compensated. Quality may be demanded from the many, or generate huge bonuses for the few, but it does not determine basic pay. The fetish made of "Quality" in corporate management is an *inverted symbolic reflection* of the way the market economy essentially undervalues quality through pay differentials based principally on symbolic, market value. The less *relative* importance quality has in determining pay, the more it is fetishised as a symbol of corporate culture, and the more it needs to be marketed and campaigned for as a management objective.

In a market economy, labour is measured only *quantitatively* – *in* clock time. Time is seen as possessing extent but not qualitative depth and breadth. The quantitative measurement and valuation of time gives all periods of labour time the same time quality and the same economic value. But the degree to which human qualities are embodied and materialised in labour, depends essentially on the *quality* of the time that workers give to each other and to their work. What Marx called the "surplus value" extracted from labour – the source of profit – is the quantitative difference between the average labour time required to produce a commodity and the labour time required to produce the goods necessary to sustain the labour power of workers. He showed that the more automated and capital intensive industry becomes, the more the general, average rate of profit actually declines. For, whilst already materialised labour time continues to be transferred from machinery and fixed assets to finished products (as the former wear out and depreciate) less new surplus value is injected into the economy from human labour itself. Companies respond by further cutting wages or "trimming" the work force, and by putting more pressure on the remaining workers and managers to increase their productivity.

Negative Quality, Time and Value

The aim of corporate cost-cutting is to defend profitability by increasing surplus value – widening the gap between the value of the labour time employees expend in work and the cost of sustaining this labour power – sustaining their capacity for work itself. But this gap is not only a quantitative one but also a qualitative one. To sustain, reproduce and enhance human labour power as a source of economic value means sustaining and enhancing the creative human qualities of individuals. This requires not only that individuals earn enough to "survive", but that they have sufficient *quality time* to sustain and enhance the human qualities they put into their work. A purely quantitative measurement of the value of labour power – average social labour hours necessary to reproduce it through the manufacture of necessary food, clothing, housing etc – does not take account of the *quality* of time necessary to sustain and enhance their individual human qualities and the individual quality of their labour.

What I call *quality time* is the product of time quantity or extent (measured objectively in social clock time) and time quality or depth (measured subjectively by individuals). What I call *negative time* is the obverse, qualitative and individual side of the "surplus labour time" that, as Marx showed, is the source of surplus value. Negative time is the difference between the amount of "quality time" individuals give to their work and the amount of quality time individuals get to replenish and enhance their creative human qualities. What I call *negative value* is the obverse, qualitative and individual side of what Marx called surplus value. It is the difference between the qualities embodied and materialised in products and services – their deep value – and the symbolic value given to these qualities in a market economy. If negative time and value increase, the result is *negative quality*. The quality of the time individuals give to their work suffers because their physical energies and creative qualities have not been replenished.

Stress is negative time – the domination of symbolic clock time over deep quality time. It is an inherent part of a market economic system which measures time only quantitatively and in which it is seen as a "scarce resource" needing to be "saved". But time cannot be properly valued except by valuing its quality as well as its quantity. Giving people *quality time* saves time by making it more fulfilling and productive. Raising labour productivity at the expense of quality time is counter-productive, generating negative value and unproductive costs – health costs in particular. To overcome stress, individuals must be able to forget deadlines and agendas and instead enter a deeper sort of time – "deep time". Normally we do this only when we sleep. But the eight-hour working day reinforces an artificial separation between our waking and working consciousness – lived under the aegis of clock time – and our creative subconscious on the other hand. This reduces the quality of the time we give to our work. We know, however, that quality itself is the result of giving tasks – and people – quality time. Innovation is not borne and good decisions are not "made" reactively – they require the subconscious digestion of information and the subconscious "incubation" of ideas, both over time and in "deep time".

Health and the Exploitation of Negative Value

Stress is embodied in sickness and poor working relationships and materialised in poor quality products, industrial accidents etc. Because, in a socialist economy, labour time would be measured and recompensed according to its quality as well as its quantity – all individuals would be ensured of sufficient compensation in labour time-and-quality credits to allow the quality time necessary to maintain their well-being, sustain their health and replenish their creative powers.

Health, mental and physical, individual and social is positive value fulfilment. Sickness, mental and physical, individual and social, human and planetary, is negative value fulfilment – the product of negative time (stress) and negative value (lack of recognition). These result in negative quality of life. The latter is not the result of illness but its cause. Every organ of the body, not just the sexual or reproductive ones, serve not merely physical but human relational functions – the heart is just as much a relational organ embodying relational qualities such as openness, love and compassion as it is a pump. In physical illness, unfulfilled human relational qualities are negatively embodied in organic dysfunction and symbolically embodied in physical symptoms. Systemic organic dysfunction becomes a *functional organising system* for human qualities that are unfulfilled in an individual's relationships. Physical symptoms serve as the embodied symbol of individual values that find no reflection in social culture. In mental illness, on the other hand, deep values are experienced in a negative and disembodied way – as obsessive negative thoughts, inner voices and hallucinations, phobias and paranoias. Objects, parts of the body, and other people become, symbolically, the negative embodiment or embodied negation of the individual's disembodied values. Behaviour that ignores or disturbs, negates or offends, exaggerates or mocks cultural norms and patterns substitutes for the positive embodiment of the individual's deep values.

Mental and physical health is dependent on "deep health" – on value fulfilment. But the less individuals feel themselves to be part of a healthy social *body* – and the less able they feel to *embody* their values in their work and relationships, the more symbolic value is placed on the health of the *physical* body as such. Whilst the pursuit of symbolic health replaces the search for deep health and value fulfilment, few resources are given to exploring and responding to the socio-somatic dimension of health problems. Little quality time is given to listening to patients and exploring the social and relational background to their symptoms. Though stress is itself the embodiment of a lack of quality time deriving from economic and ethical value exploitation, the word "stress" becomes the universal blanket term by which to avoid having to heed the embodied symbolism of physical disease. Indeed, the very idea that symptoms may have a symbolic character is taken to imply that they have no organic basis at all, thus wasting the GP's time. GPs, after all, are themselves "under stress". The few minutes available for each patient do not encourage people to speak intimately. They are aware from the minute they enter the consulting room that their time is running out, and that the doctor's listening has its own very clear and bounded agenda – restricted to letting the patient talk *about* their symptoms – but not to hear them speak. The medical agenda is restricted to incorporating the patient's bodily symptoms into the body of medical symbols and terminology, and to ignoring their embodied symbolism, physical and behavioural. As a result, medical practitioners become, in attending to their patients' minds and bodies, the very model of the impatient and mentally disembodied listener.

The phrase "to treat a patient" becomes the best definition of what it means not to listen patiently and really hear. The claim that GPs cannot "afford" to give more quality time to each patient is the clearest example of how quality of time is confused with quantity. But the consequent rationing of health expenditure – both in time and money – is self-defeating. For patients then end up needing longer sessions with consultants or costing the health services huge amounts as their condition aggravates. Waiting lists and a waiting room full of patients thus become the symbol of a capitalist social culture in which the knowing expert – *homo sapiens* – dominates *homo patiens* – the capacity to patiently wait upon ourselves and others.

Most people do not go to medical practitioners for pills and treatments, nor even for placebos and diagnostic labels to reduce their anxiety. Though both these motives might apply on the surface they are *ersatz* motives conditioned by the rules of the language game played out between doctor and patient. The real reason people go to a GP is to *be heard*. Not having found a way of being heard in their own families or workplace their body speaks for them – providing through its symptoms a wordless set of embodied symbols as an alternative to the words that have so far failed – an alternative language. The denial of the symbolic and socio-somatic dimensions of health, and the reduction of social distress to individual "stress", keeps the profits of the health industry, in all its forms, rolling in. In this respect the privatisation of health-care provision merely symbolises the *de facto* privatisation of "health" and "illness" as such – their reduction to the accidental flaws of the individual's physiology or genes. This soulless reductionism fosters nothing but the health of pharmaceutical companies. Its salesmen are the major legal drug pushers on the market today. But only in a fundamentally unhealthy society can medical drugs, vitamins and complementary health fads become such a booming commodity. Only in a fundamentally unhealthy society can Health itself become such a viral fetish as it is now – a "health bug". Only in a market economy can both health and sickness become a source of economic exploitation, the exploitation of negative value and negative value fulfilment.

The introduction of the internal market in the National Health System shows only too well the failure of capitalist costing criteria. When preventative health units are closed down as poor investments despite the massive overall economic cost savings these could bring to the nation, the economic logic of a socialist planned economy becomes plain to see. But a truly radical socialist health policy would not merely concern itself with the economic funding of national health care, and the quantity of patients that can be treated. Instead it must address the very *nature* of health, health care and health care "quality".

Negative Value and Deep Costs

Right-wing critics of unlimited government spending on health are right, even though they offend their own principles when they argue it: money isn't everything. The deep health of individuals and society can never be ensured or *insured* in a market economy and a culture of marketing and value exploitation. Capitalism can only move forward by limiting the economic health costs that result, at whatever cost to society. The same is true of environmental costs resulting from the exploitation of nature. Surplus value is extracted not only economically from human labour, but ecologically – from natural resources. Surplus value extracted from nature is the difference between the time required to extract, package and distribute, from natural resources and the time required to sustain and *reproduce* those resources. Faster extraction, packaging, distribution and consumption of resources increases surplus value and short-term profit, but reduces the time given for the natural reproduction of resources as well as interfering with this reproduction through environmental damage. This produces the same embodiment of "negative value" in the body of the planet as it does in individuals, creating a "sick planet". It reduces the earth to a dumping ground for toxic waste, the sea to a vast fish farm, plants, animals and even humans to genetic livestock. Yet a society that treats non-human beings not as living beings but as raw materials to be "processed" in industrial concentration camps will always be capable of doing the same to human beings.

In a market economy there is a disguised and perverse symbolic ambiguity in the use of such phrases as "environmental costs", "health costs", "costs of unemployment" etc. For whilst they are used to refer to the measurable economic costs *of* environmental damage, sickness, unemployment etc. they merely allude to the *immeasurable* costs of environmental damage *to* the environment itself, the immeasurable costs of sickness *to* the sick, the immeasurable costs of unemployment *to* the unemployed etc. The impression is given that measurable economic costs are more "real" than immeasurable human or ecological ones, whilst at the same time tacitly admitting that the latter have something to do with the former. In fact these economic costs are the merely symbolic, quantitative expression of deep qualitative costs – costs to the quality of life, quality of society, quality of culture and quality of environment. They are negative unproductive costs economically, and the qualitative expressions of negative value. The word "cost" itself conceals the distinction between deep and symbolic costs, qualitative and quantitative costs, costs which are a quantitative expression of positive value creation, and costs which are the qualitative embodiment and materialisation of negative value creation. There is, of course, an economic price to pay for deep costs: a price to pay for not really listening to people, for example, or of ignoring or devaluing their qualities and potentials. A price to pay for creating a demoralised work force through over-rapid organisational change, "downsizing" or pay freezes. A price to pay for not thinking deeply enough about long-term issues, of not taking one's time over decisions and tasks, of not giving quality time to oneself and others.

The trouble with many of these "intangible" costs is not that they are intangible, since for most people they are the most tangible costs of all – costs, which are directly experienced, and against which mere economic statistics pale into abstraction. The problem is that a market economy places its own intangible, purely quantitative costs over these tangible, deep costs, and only takes account of the latter when they express themselves symbolically in a measurable way. That is why, even in referring to "environmental costs", "health costs", "crime costs" or to the "costs of unemployment" they have in mind short-, medium- or long-term economic costs: the eventual economic cost of decommissioning a nuclear power station that is past its use-by date, the costs of cleaning up polluted waters, the costs of paying for the effects of widespread social-somatic stress on the population through the health services, policing and prisons. The paradox is, of course, that these *added* and unwelcome economic costs are themselves the symbolic expression of an obsession with *reducing* economic costs – one which has the effect of stressing the environment for the sake of profit, stressing employees for the sake of productivity, and of stressing social health through the very cuts that are imposed on health provision. This is the vicious circle of "monetarism" and "economism", the ideologies that reflect and guide the global market economy.

Work, Jobs and Deep Employment

What most people seek is deep employment. This does not mean simply having a "job", even a "good job". It means *doing* a good job — one in which they embody and fulfil their human qualities to the utmost in their work. The number of people willing to commit themselves to unpaid voluntary work and "do gooding" is a symbol of this basic desire. The search for deep employment is dampened less by *no-pay* than by low-pay, low-recognition jobs of the sort that the labour market offers the unemployed and social security agencies pressure them to take up. The reduction of unemployment statistics that comes about in this way, irrespective of how they are calculated, is a symbolic one only. The deep, qualitative unemployment of human potentials remains – with all its deep costs. Those who are not in paid work are not by any means necessarily unoccupied or idle. Instead they tend to occupy themselves with a whole range of unpaid activities that have little or no market value, whether domestic or voluntary work, creative or learning activities, caring for relatives or children. To see them as contributing nothing to society is a complete devaluation of these activities; a social attitude which is the main cause of depression and demoralisation in the unemployed. But those in work suffer similar demoralisation through the devaluation, under-recognition and unemployment of their human qualities, skills and potentials.

Clerical, liberal and left wing moralists may bemoan high statistical unemployment and its costs, both economic and human. Liberal economists and managers may "regret" the mass redundancies made "necessary" by the market economy. What they fail to see, however, is that high statistical unemployment is merely the inevitable, cyclical expression of a deep unemployment that constantly pervades capitalist society, devaluing and demoralising those in and out of work. The employed are urged to value the work they have, however much it exploits the value of their labour and devalues the qualities they bring to it. The unemployed are promised that the market economy can give them a job if they really want it, but only so long as they don't want too much from it. The unemployed are "released" from economic value exploitation only to be educationally exploited through a retraining that aims to make their labour power once again into a marketable commodity, and to turn their social behaviour into the embodied symbol of a "good" employee.

Deep unemployment affects more than just the unemployed. Studies in Germany* have shown that young people attracted to neo-Nazi groups do not, by and large, come from the underclass or the unemployed but from middle class families. What unites them is their attitude to work, which they see only as a means to an end and not as a medium of value recognition and fulfilment. This view is, of course, encouraged by situations of high "real" unemployment which force people to seek jobs rather than deep employment. And yet it also reflects the deep unemployment of those who are in fact in paid work. Sensing this, young people seek recognition and fulfilment in the deep values and deep value kinships that link people in relationships, ethnic groups and youth sub-cultures. The fact that neo-Nazi youth identify such deep value kinships with racist symbols and ideologies, whereas most others use drugs or more innocent forms of symbolic behaviour to express, embody or act out their values symbolically makes no essential difference. This is an unhealthy and dangerous situation, produced not because of the decline of the so-called "work ethic" but as a result of it. For this ethic is not the ethic of hard work but the ethic of hard work as a sacrifice for an employer or shareholder, as a means to an end.

Deep unemployment is not only positive quantitative unemployment figures. It is also negative qualitative employment – the production of negative value and negative costs. Negative employment is the basis of positive unemployment. Conversely positive unemployment may transform itself into negative employment, not just in the form of unfulfilling low paid work but in the form of crime, fraud, arms manufacture, war and other forms of negative value manufacture. Nazism transformed high positive unemployment and the devaluation of human beings through the market economy into planned negative employment and manufacture of negative value. It transformed people's deep sense of devaluation and demoralisation, into a positive affirmation of purely symbolic values, represented by the swastika. In this it created a social political model for the commercial culture of marketing, which transforms the lack of deep value fulfilment into a positive drive for symbolic value fulfilment through the brand symbol. It also created the model for modern corporate symbolism based on the company logo, and for the transformation of deep employment into *symbolic employment* – uniformed, regimented and "rationalised" employment in the service of corporate symbols, competition and profit. Symbolic employment is not the same as negative employment. Deep employment can also be expressed in symbols and symbolic values. But where symbolic value fulfilment becomes a substitute for deep value fulfilment, symbolic employment tends to the manufacture of negative value – until it destroys itself.

Modern corporate crime exceeds all household or street crime. What Michael Moore has called corporate terrorism – inflicting life long unemployment on communities, or life long negative employment on those in low pay, low recognition and low fulfilment work is a manufacture of negative value in the service of symbolic value and shareholder gain. So, indeed, is the manufacture of arms and their supply to regimes violating human rights. The manufacture of negative value is self-rationalising. The more arms, the more instability, the more the need for armies, the bigger the arms market. If we don't sell them, others will, goes the argument with the unassailable logic of the market economy. This logic is the logic of submission to the market and its forces justified in the name of competition – of jobs for our boys. So also is war a submission to violence, justified by the need to protect the lives of our people. This belief in the superior worth of "our" people's lives or jobs, houses or culture was also more than echoed in "National Socialism" — the most extreme form of National Capitalism.

* Heitmeyer, Wilhelm. *Rechtsextremistische Orientierungen bei Jugendlichen.* München. Juventa 1992.

Educational Value Exploitation

The value of education cannot be reduced to its usefulness in passing exams, learning technical skills or getting a job. To the extent that it is, the nature and value of human knowledge is fundamentally misunderstood, and with it, the intrinsic value of learning. Sounds can be electronically represented in the form of wave patterns on an oscilloscope, but that does not mean that it makes sense to say sound "is" or "consists of" such wave patterns. For sound is essentially something that we sense and respond to in a bodily way, that we hear, jump or dance to, modulate in our speech and make as music. Sine waves or the vibrational patterns of air molecules are things that we may plot and display, visualise or measure – ie, represent symbolically. To ignore this crucial categorical distinction in education is to risk imposing on children a basic confusion between explicit *symbolic knowledge* in the form of words and pictures, diagrams and explanations and implicit, *embodied knowledge* in the form of sensual bodily activity and awareness.

Doing a classroom experiment in physics may be a valuable experience for children in learning to manipulate instruments and take readings. But the values and readings they record are purely symbolic values – a temperature reading or a weight measurement. Recording and charting them does not teach children to read and value their experience of the basic phenomena under investigation, to discover the similarity-in-difference and difference-in-similarity between their own experience and that of others. It forces them to work with the abstract intellectual products of human sensual activity – with representational concepts and images – but it does not cultivate their sensual, bodily experience of this activity, their sensual, bodily awareness of the inner processes of thinking, feeling and willing. As a result, whilst their scientific knowledge, mathematical and technical skills may (or may not) improve, they do not learn to value, symbolise and learn from their own experience but are trained instead to distrust and devalue it. They come to depend on symbols and concepts provided by others, or simply on those already embedded in current idioms, jargons and phraseologies of the capitalist culture.

Symbolic knowledge of sound may be extremely relevant to the manufacture of stereo equipment, loudspeakers or ultra-sound scanners, but it does not cultivate enrichment of the child's embodied knowledge of sound, as for example, music and dance education do. Nor does it in any way directly symbolise this embodied knowledge, but instead imposes its own symbols and terminology on it. Education based principally on symbolic knowledge essentially teaches children to separate the symbols and scientific concepts with which we represent phenomena – whether light or sound, gravity or heat – from their intimate felt sense of those phenomena. It trains them to value the agreed symbolic "senses" of words more than their own bodies and feelings. This is an educational form of *value exploitation*, for whilst symbolic education indirectly relies and feeds off a child's embodied knowledge and sensual experience, what it gives them back is symbols denuded of living, experiential value. It does e-ducate ("lead out") the individual quality of each child's experience and helps them to articulate and symbolise this. If language itself is reduced to an instrument of international commerce or a set of techniques for getting through a job interview, it is no wonder that children leave school inarticulate or emotionally illiterate, ignorant of the richness of their language.

To develop a socialist education policy and system is impossible without radically questioning the essential nature of education in capitalist society, and the way it privileges symbolic knowledge for its own purposes. The "life-long learning" vaunted by advocates of short-term "flexible" employment means, in reality, life-long dependency on academic concepts and vocational skills handed down from above; life-long educational value exploitation designed to serve the market exploitation of labour. Socialist education is *deep education* with a deep and long term value, rather than purely symbolic education with a purely symbolic value – certificates and job earnings. Deep education does not mean concentrating education on the arts and humanities, as against science and technology. Its aim is to develop what Marx called a "human science of nature" and a "natural science of man", one which does not demand that children – or adults – devalue their living experience of the world and surrender it to symbols that have no living relation to this experience and which do not help them to articulate it and learn from it. Deep education is an education that encourages learners to explore their own human, bodily experience of natural phenomena and their own sensual bodily experience of human phenomena – of human relationships, qualities, values and ideas. Its aim is not the training and "socialisation" of a technically skilled and independent but emotionally, intellectually and politically dependent corporate work force. Its aim is the cultivation of socially aware individuals who trust and value their own sensual bodily experience, their feelings and intuitions, and who can therefore both articulate their own ideas and truly embody their own values.

Most science teachers would of course agree that our sensual experience of sound is not the same thing as the science of sound. Yet they might still argue that hearing is merely a result of cause and effect, a "subjective" phenomenon produced by the "laws of physics". This scientistic view is quite unscientific, for it reduces human sensual experience of natural phenomena to a symbolic representation of this experience in terms of "laws" and "forces", terms which themselves derive from human social and bodily experience. To develop a "human science of nature" and "a natural science" of man, means above all, to explore the social and bodily symbolism of language itself, not only literary language but scientific language, not only concrete language but abstract academic language. The word "abstract" itself derives from bodily experience (*abstrahere* – to lift off). Education cannot promote deep intellectual or artistic creativity by teaching abstract concepts "lifted" from human social activity and sensual experience, if divorced from this activity and experience whilst appropriating it for other purposes. The only culture which *this* model of intellectual and artistic creativity fits is the culture of marketing. The only society which values intellectual products of this sort is one based on value exploitation of creative human labour and the labour of creativity.

Marx for Managers

In the Communist Manifesto Marx described how social change comes about when formal social relations – particularly relations of production, ownership and control, lag behind the development of the "forces of production" – industrial technology. Formal social relations are "vertical" relations based on chains of ownership, control of resources and capital, on hierarchical relationships of status, authority and pay. They are fundamentally asymmetric relations, such as those that exist between owners and managers, managers and staff. These must be distinguished from "horizontal" relationships between individuals, peers and members of the same social class or profession. Although in Japanese culture these tend to be subsumed under vertical relations of rank and status, this distinction remains fundamental. Horizontal relations are the dimension that the Jewish social thinker Martin Buber called "the inter human". He saw the inter human as central to the cultural life and creativity of any company, collective or community, arguing that it is not the formal structures and social relations of a group that generate this creativity, nor the qualities embodied by its individual members, but the quality of their human relationships.

It is because social relations are inseparable from deep human relations that so-called "Human Relations Management" eventually began to take an important role in corporate life, and that so-called "inter-personal skills" are now called for in most management job descriptions and cultivated in management training. HRM has played a particular role in bringing about necessary revolutions in corporate structures – the flattening of management hierarchies, the greater use of teamwork etc. And yet these revolutions in corporate culture and structure are often superficial and merely symbolic. Where they have been successful in a radical and deep-seated way, they have introduced a much stronger element of cooperative human relations – of socialist culture – into corporate life. The question remains, however: are changes in corporate culture pursued as ends-in-themselves, or only as means to achieve greater productivity, profit and growth? The more the latter is the case, the greater the skepticism of the work force and the more superficial and cosmetic the changes that are made. The more the former is the case, the more authentic are the changes that result – and the more they threaten the principles of "return on capital" and "shareholder value".

Workers and staff are always keenly aware of the "value climate" of the workplace; of the human qualities embodied – or not embodied – by individuals in industrial relations, working relationships and departmental life. In so far as managers are also individual employees and not merely profiteering shareholders, they too seek value fulfilment as well as "results". Their function as mediators between a value system which privileges symbolic values and one which seeks to fulfil deep values is thus often an important one. Profit itself is a symbolic value only – a symbolic expression either of value fulfilment or of value exploitation. Collectives in a socialist economy would also generate surplus value. To whatever extent, surplus value is turned into an end in itself however, it becomes the expression not of collective value fulfilment but of value exploitation and *negative value*. Value fulfilment alone generates positive surplus value – deep profit – because it derives from human relationships in which individuals value one another and therefore derive value from one another – learn from each other's qualities and help each other to embody and materialise them. The democratic socialist transformation of corporate management, objectives and strategy – the creation of a deep and value generating industrial democracy – requires a culture based on dialogue and relational learning. Relational learning, the capacity to value and learn from others, is the basis of both ethics and education, for ethics is about learning to value others and education is about valuing what we learn from others.

Individuals, teams, departments and companies can often only acknowledge and fulfil their deep values by symbolic reflection. Relational learning means valuing the words and actions of *other* individuals, teams, departments and companies, including customers and suppliers (however much one disagrees with or dislikes them) as a symbolic reflection (however disguised or distorted) of human qualities that we have not yet fully expressed or embodied ourselves. Only by valuing other people's way of doing things can we learn something from them, take them on board and derive value from them. Only by learning from and taking on board other people's ways of doing do we learn to value them fully.

A culture of relational learning is not achieved by clever management, training seminars or fashionable New Age management jargons. It cannot be reduced to superficial corporate "value statements" or cosmetic transformations of corporate culture. A culture of relational learning is not a tool of human relations management or corporate marketing. It is a cultural revolution in the deepest, most radical socialist sense. Beyond the ethics and economics of the market, and beyond the culture of "marketing" and of "management" as we know it.

As it is, management thinking, however, tends to be bound up with the purely quantitative symbolic values represented by bullet points and graphs, strategies and slogans, quarterly reports and budgets. In so far as managers see themselves as serving the interest of shareholders, including themselves, their thinking is dominated by these symbolic values — by profit. Yet as employees they are also caught between a value system which privileges symbolic values and one which seeks to fulfil deep values. Yet without deep industrial democracy and the step-by-step transformation of corporations, the power of individual managers is limited — unless they also support such a transformation. Management thinking makes no distinction between positive and negative surplus value, profit maximisation and deep profit maximisation. The pay differentials of the market economy have their foundation in a model of social and inter human relations in which each person competes with others for value recognition and value fulfilment, and in which self-worth is sustained only by overvaluing or undervaluing the qualities of others. Only the socialist transformation of corporate structure and culture can create an economy in which the rationally planned production and satisfaction of material needs, and the generation of surplus value is the result not of the value exploitation of individuals but of their mutual, relational value fulfilment.

The Symbolic Democracy of Capitalism

The moralisation of politics goes hand in hand with the marketing of political parties and leaders and their policies and "values" to the electorate. The latter are treated merely as consumers of moral values and economic value rather than as value producers. This increasing commodification of parties, persons and policies, which need to be "sold" to the electorate on the basis of their symbolic moral and economic value, reflects the fundamental gulf that exists in a capitalist democracy between symbolic politics and real politics, political symbolism and policy decisions, parties and real people.

People respond to the issues raised in political debate, not only according to the real impact of different policies on their lives (something which is anyway inevitably disguised or distorted by political marketing) but according to what these issues symbolise for them. Any given group of people who "support" the same policies may do so for quite different reasons, because the issues concerned symbolise different things for different people. Conversely, people, including politicians, who take different or opposing positions on the same issue may do so out of similar motives. Political leaders and personalities are chosen and elected, not principally on the basis of their calculated symbolic behaviour, their espoused values and policies, but because the particular combinations of human qualities they embody are valued more than those of their rivals. These embodied qualities are also interpreted and evaluated by different people in terms with their own symbolic values. Policies symbolise the deep values people wish to embody and materialise in their real lives. They are also symbolic interpretations of these deep values, shaped by deep political beliefs.

The greater the gulf between symbolic values and real behaviour of politicians, between what issues and policies symbolise for people and the effects they have on people's real lives, the greater the gulf between symbolic politics and real politics. This gulf is not the "fault" of politicians. It is itself the political symbol of a social gulf between people's deep values and the way they symbolise these values in words and deeds, speech and behaviour. As such it is an expression of the market economy itself, whose intrinsic tendency is to turn symbolic values into ends in themselves, and into commodities – whilst voiding them of substance. The symbolic politics of capitalist democracy can be used to promote social democrats and the "social market" but it provides no direct route to democratic socialism. It can serve socialism only as the indirect expression of radical social transformation taking place at the "grass roots." Socialist politics is not just real as opposed to symbolic politics. It is also deep politics. Deep politics requires a deep understanding not only of real issues but of the symbolic dimension of the political process itself. For this is but one expression of the dialectics of value(s) – the relation between deep and symbolic values. Such insight can then be embodied in new and deeper forms of political activity, based not on symbols, but on the real relations of committed individuals.

Currencies, Languages and the National "Ethos"

Currencies are the symbolic languages of commercial exchange. Languages are the symbolic currencies of communicative exchange. Different currencies have a different quantitative exchange value, which expresses their material purchasing power, so do languages. Different languages give us a different qualitative "purchase" on meaning. By "different language", however, we have to understand not only different national tongues but different phraseologies and terminologies, and the *ideologies* these express. Grammar and vocabulary are not merely the constituents of a given language. For, simply using different terms and phrases to express the "same" thing is to recast our meaning entirely, to employ a different language. The myth that the same thing can be said in different ways, with no effect on meaning – on our relationship to what is spoken of and our relationship to those we address – is an expression of the illusion created by the process of communicative exchange. Wherever there is real listening, we hear through someone's words to their embodied and material meaning – their dialogical meaning and not merely the shared meaning of their words. To the extent that we listen dialogically, however, we hear something else too. We hear the way in which their relational bearing is itself shaped by the typical words, terms and phrases they employ, how it has become, itself, the symbolic embodiment and materialisation of their own typical language.

If the nature of money is understood dialectically, there is no such thing as a "common currency". Common trans-national currencies, like common ideologies, are an integral part of the market economy, not just because they are practical but because of the differences they conceal. A national currency is itself a "common currency", a trans-regional currency concealing real differences in the purchasing power of money in different regions. The creation of common trans-national currencies abolishes only the symbolic manifestation of real differences in exchange rates. These will then simply find other forms of symbolic manifestation – in price and pay levels for example. The creation of common national or ideological languages abolishes only the symbolic differences between individuals. These will simply find other forms of manifestation – in differences of register and dialect, or in the type of contrasting verbal nuancing that journalists look for in the statements of politicians from the same party.

Languages, like currencies, nevertheless have a symbolic value, which transcends their practical symbolic use and their exchange value in commerce and communication. This deep symbolic value lies in the way they express embodied and material meanings, the relationships of a group or people to each other and the world. The use of English as a common linguistic currency of trade and commerce, for example, by no means abolishes the different *ways of relating* embodied by speakers whose first language is not English. These only find symbolic expression in their own native tongue. And yet if the nature of language is understood dialogically, the idea of a common linguistic currency is as much an illusion as the idea of a common economic currency.

Communication is meaningful not because the same words are used to "mean the same things" but because they are used to mean different things – because our relationships to those things is different. It is this difference that communicates through our words, even if not in them. It is the difference-in-similarity between different people's use of the same word that allows it to communicate *their* meaning and not just *its* meaning. It is the difference-in-similarity between supposedly equivalent words in one language – or supposedly equivalent words in two languages – that make foreign languages meaningful as well as useful.

Common languages only appear to abolish real differences of meaning in the way individuals use words. Their deep value is to create a flexible *body* of symbols that allows the communication of deep embodied meanings and deep values – of individual meanings and relational qualities. Common currencies only abolish economic differences between regions and nations symbolically, by eliminating exchange rates. These differences then become symbolically manifest in a more direct economic way, through price and pay levels. But if nations possess a distinct currency *as well as* a distinct language, the currency itself is imbued with a deep symbolic value of the same character as that of the language. It is seen as the symbol of relational qualities and styles – the *ethos* of a culture. The connection between national languages and national currencies is not merely a symbolic one, however. The relational qualities of a people, symbolised in language, behavioural patterns and expressed "values" is also materialised in their social and working relationships, and in the functioning of their economy. Therefore, if the symbolic behaviour and cultural symbols of a people, their social and human relations, are themselves a disguised or distorted expression of their human relational qualities – their deep values and deep *ethos* – then the abandonment of a national currency, like the abandonment of a national language takes on a deep symbolic meaning. For, like the abandonment of a national language, it is seen as depriving them of the *symbolic* connection to this *ethos*. This is the symbolic meaning of the political debate over European Monetary Union.

Fears of loss of national identity, values and ethos, are intrinsic to the capitalist market economy and its culture of marketing, which both reinforces the idea that these values are its private property, and yet in so doing, make them hypothetically exchangeable for any other. Today, the private property of individuals and nations is not their deep values and ethos, but only the symbolic expression of these values in words, money and behaviour. Deep values are not lost by abandoning particular symbols, indeed, the process allows new and deeper symbols to emerge.

Part 2

Moral Education
or
Relational Learning?

The Dialectics of Value(s)

Who is wise? He who learns from all...
The Talmud

Individuality and the Market in Values

Moral education is traditionally linked to values such as "respect", "tolerance", "loyalty", "courage", "honesty", "compassion" etc. These values are essentially human qualities, qualities which individuals embody in *relating* to each other and the world, to non-human beings, and to things. Particular human relational qualities are seen as "moral qualities" when they are highly valued or regarded as being of fundamental value by particular individuals, groups and cultures. These valued qualities are symbolised in words and images, codes of behaviour and religious icons. In this way they become the "shared values" of groups and communities. But the very process by which cultures symbolise human qualities and translate them into shared, symbolic values invariably disguises their individual quality. For different people embody different *qualities* of "sincerity", "courage", "compassion" etc. Paradoxically, therefore, no words that we use to represent and symbolise embodied personal qualities can ever fully communicate the individual way in which these qualities are embodied – their individual quality. By naming an individual's personal qualities in words, we both designate them as the *property* of that person and reduce them to common property, a "shared value".

For, each of the words we use could equally well be assigned to other individuals. "Valuing" a person's qualities can mean two things, therefore. It can mean that we perceive and value them in their individual quality, or that we value them as shared qualities – ones we can symbolise. Valuing a person's qualities deeply means valuing them not just as exchangeable qualities which happen to be "possessed" by that individual but valuing them in their *individual quality*, the unique way in which that person embodies them. Valuing a person symbolically, on the other hand, means valuing their individual qualities only as the symbolic expression of nameable and exchangeable qualities, of "shared values". Traditional "moral education" has to do with such shared symbolic values only. These include cultural symbols, words and images, and symbolic behaviour. Symbolic behaviour is embodied symbolism, including speech and body language. But the deep value of the individual qualities that people embody in their relationships cannot be reduced to symbolic behaviour, cannot be reduced to their symbolic values and do not stem from "moral education" in these values. What makes individuals valuable is not the shared values they "hold" or "have", not their symbolic "be-have-iour", but the individual qualities that they embody and communicate through it. Not what they do but the way that they do it. These are embodied in their human activity – their individual way of doing things. It is this that links *what* they do to who they *are*, for the essence of an individual's self-being is their way of being, embodied in their way of doing.

In cultures dominated by symbolic values, people value their individual qualities and those of others only as a symbolic expression of shared values. They value others for doing it their way, whether "their" way means "our" way or "my way". People's behaviour is seen as either conforming to or defying the symbolic behaviour valued by that culture. Individuals thus tend to value each other's embodied qualities only in so far as these embody and reflect their own symbolic values. Behaviour is reduced to embodied symbolism – to behaviour that symbolises group value systems. People value each other only for *what* they do and say and not for *how* they do or say it. Whilst each person seeks to be valued for *who* they are and *how* they do things they compete for this deep value recognition by attempting to prove their worth to others in purely symbolic terms – either complying with each other's beliefs and behaviour or countering them with their own. Here lies a central paradox. For the truism that "we all need to be valued" only *becomes* true because people do not fully value their own individual qualities and way of doing things, but instead surrender them to the desire for symbolic value recognition and reward from others – for "success".

The type of communication that results is dominated by the dynamics of commodity exchange. In the process of commercial exchange, the material use-value of commodities becomes merely the outward expression of a purely symbolic value: their exchange value symbolised in money. In the process of communicative exchange, what is communicated through a person's words becomes merely the outward expression of a purely symbolic value: the exchange value of these words as conventional symbols. The embodied qualities of individuals are valued principally as the behavioural embodiment of their symbolic value – their conformity with personal or group norms. Commodity exchange reduces the sensual and material qualities of products to their value in commercial exchange – their standard monetary value. Communicative exchange reduces the embodied and material meaning of words (how they communicate the speaker's real relationship to both the person and matter addressed) to their value in communicative exchange – their standard social meaning. In commercial exchange people buy each other's products in the form of commodities – but only according to the exchange value of these commodities. Products without exchange value are seen as commercially valueless. In communicative exchange people buy each other's thoughts and feelings in the form of words – but only as these are shaped by the given meaning of their words. Meanings that defy words are seen as meaningless and valueless – even though they are the essence of what communicates *through* the word.

Money is the medium of commercial exchange. Language is the medium of communicative exchange. Currencies are the languages of commercial exchange. Languages are the currencies of "communicative exchange". When relationships operate merely at the level of communicative exchange, people tend to devalue each other's individual qualities if they are not offered for sale in the right currency, do not conform to their own behavioural symbolism and language. People confront each other like buyers willing to purchase each other's goods, but only if they are made to their own specifications and can be paid in their currency. Each person seeks to "sell" their own human qualities and way of doing things to others, by conforming to quality specifications set by others and accepting symbolic reward in the currency of others. Moreover they interpret each other's words and actions in terms of their own symbolic value system. They do not value each other's embodied qualities except as the embodied reflection of their own symbolic value system, they *evaluate* each other's symbolic behaviour, judging its conformity to their own.

The Dialectical Principle of Simference

Though each person wants others to see through their own outward, symbolic behaviour and "be valued for who they are", their embodied qualities, each looks to the other for a reflection of their own symbolic values – for what they are. An intrinsic dependency on others for basic value recognition, the acknowledgement of their self-worth, goes hand in hand with an inverted narcissism – a deficient self-esteem and self-love. People do not use each other as a mirror of themselves. They use each other as a mirror of the symbolic values in which they clothe themselves. They do not seek a reflection of their self-worth but of their symbolic worth.

Under conditions of capitalist mass production, the process of commercial exchange leads to standardisation. Everyone seeks to produce and sell to the same qualitative standards, competing with each other only to meet these standards to the highest possible quantitative degree. This puts an inherent brake on qualitative innovation. Similarly, in a mass culture governed by communicative exchange, each individual must compete to conform to cultural values and symbolic behaviours to the highest possible degree, if they want to succeed. The impetus to commercial conformity and standardisation is felt to be a power in itself. It is called The Market and codified in the rules of business – in "how to succeed". The impetus to conform to standardised symbolic behaviour is also felt to be a power in itself. It is called God, and codified in religious laws. But both God and The Market are themselves human symbols of a deep and divine power that they devalue in themselves – the power to create their own reality by embodying and materialising their human qualities in their own way without competing for "success" in symbolic, market terms.

This power and these qualities, however, do not lend themselves to expression through the common currencies of religious, moral and business language. They are neither private property nor common property, for they are relational qualities. They can be understood dialectically, not as similarities or differences between people but as "similarities-in-difference" – *simferences*. Neither the traditional moral cliche that as human beings "we're all the same underneath", nor the fashionable "post-modern" emphasis on the Difference and Otherness of others acknowledge the dialectics of simference in human relations.

If two individuals were alike in every respect they would not be two but one – there could be no relationship between them. If two individuals were different in every respect there would be no way in which they could relate to each other. This does not mean that individuals are alike "in certain respects" and different in others. Were this to be the case, they would also bear no relation to one another. For in the respects in which they were similar, they would be absolutely similar and therefore indistinguishable as individuals. And in the respects in which they were different they would be absolutely different, and therefore absolutely incomparable. Individuals, then, are not simply alike in certain ways and different in others. Rather, they are more or less *simferent* in any given respect. Simferences cannot be reduced to similarities "and" differences, or to similarities "or" differences. A simference is a difference between people that is manifest in the very ways in which they are most similar to one another, or, conversely, a similarity that is manifest in the ways they are most different. Simferences can be compared to family resemblances — similarities in their features which do not abolish difference. And yet, to say that someone "has" their mother's eyes or "has" their father's "determination", is to represent these features merely as similarities, and to ignore simference. The principle of simference explains why the fiercest rows often take place in couples, families and communities with the strongest relationships and most intense bonds. It also explains why religious and political organisations, despite their moral principles and symbolic values, often split into warring factions which hate each other more than their joint opponents. So long as relationships, groups and organisations are formed only on the basis of *shared* values, or of opposition to groups and organisations with *different* values, they will sooner or later come up against the reality of simference – discovering ignored differences amongst themselves and ignored similarities with their opponents.

What I call "deep values" are the qualitative simferences linking the qualities embodied by one individual with those of others, or linking the qualities embodied in the relationship of two or more individuals with those embodied in the inter human relationships of other groups of individuals. If two or more individuals value a simference between them, they share what I call a "deep value kinship". This may or may not be expressed through a set of shared symbolic values. Yet all traditional symbolic value systems, social and religious, ethnic and cultural, have their origin in deep value kinships. The modern culture of marketing, however, is not simply a new modern and eclectic culture, but a "post-modern" inversion of all previous cultures. It is not a multi-culture but a "post-culture", transforming all deep value kinships into spiritual commodities.

In social relations based on the understanding of values, language and behaviour as private property, two moral messages compete. One moral message is "Do what we do." The rider to this one is "If you don't, you're doing (it) wrong." The other is "I'll do what I want to do." One message emphasises traditional "shared values", the other "individual" ones. But these so-called "individual" values, by the very fact that they are treated as private property which individuals "sell" to each other as "their" values, are no less "shared" than the traditional ones. And these "shared values", by the very fact that they are held as the symbolic stock-in-trade of religions and political parties, corporations and nations, are no less "private property" than the individual values they oppose. Moral education based on shared symbolic value systems competes with a shallow and inverted "individualism" based on freely selecting one's own symbolic values from the market place. "Do what we do" and "I'll do what I want" are not two contradictory moral positions. They are the twin expressions of the market economy. "Do what we do" is the message of symbolic value producers. It reads "Buy what we sell – ours goods are the only true Good." "I'll do what I want" is the message of symbolic value consumers. It reads "I'll buy what I want – and make a new good to sell to others." The bourgeois "crisis of moral values" is a haggle in values.

The Fetishism of Moral Phraseology

The fetishism of the phrase "family values" is a devaluation of the value of each and every family. The values of an English middle-class Christian family are not the same as those of a German middle-class Christian family, a working class Afro-Caribbean family, or an immigrant Jewish socialist family. Above all, each family is no less unique and "eccentric" culturally than it is genetically. Its "family values" cannot be reduced to values shared with other families, to race or religions, stereotyped cultural symbols and behaviours. If "respect for family values" means anything it can only mean the ability to acknowledge and respect the eccentricities and peculiarities of each family, for it is in these that its deep values are often symbolically embodied. Nor can the deep value kinships or "resemblances" connecting members of a family be reduced either to nature or nurture, to inherited genes or inherited cultural or behavioural symbolism. For, it is in the very ways in which family members resemble one another most closely that they also express and embody important differences.

Deep values are based not on similarity or difference but on similarity-in-difference: on "simference". It is simference that ensures the creative transmutation and transformation of their genetic and cultural inheritance from one generation to the next. This transmutation and transformation does not come about through family members manipulating each other's genes or abandoning their value kinships. It comes about through their combining, embodying and expressing their "moral genes" in new ways. Each member of the family draws upon a pool of deep values, just as they draw upon the family's gene pool. Different family members embody different elements or combinations of elements from this pool, and express them in different ways.

Describing human qualities using moral phraseology is one way in which the deep values embodied by individuals in their relationships are translated into shared symbols – symbolic values. Shared patterns and codes of behaviour are another. By behaving in a way that *symbolises* a "shared value" we do not necessarily embody the human quality it represents. Instead we embody the symbols of that quality. Symbolic behaviour is *embodied symbolism*, expressed through gestures, moral codes and "body language". These share the same generic, stereotypical character as moral terms and phrases – concealing individual qualities that people embody in their relationships. Indeed, individuals and families can and do embody particular relational qualities without any need of symbols to represent them or stereotyped behaviour to signal, codify or ritualise them. Value fulfilment is not achieved by submerging oneself in a group or community and identifying with its symbolic values or moral code. Nor is moral character developed by isolating oneself from society and disidentifying from all symbolic values. It is realised through the capacity to appreciate the deep values underlying the cultural, verbal and behavioural symbolism of others, even though the latter may be a disguised or distorted translation of the former.

Values, Genes and Multiculturalism

To talk about "individual values" or "social values", "Judaeo-Christian values" or "Muslim values", "English values" or "German values" is to imply that such values are the private property of individuals, groups, ethnic cultures or nations. If so however, then pluralism and multi-cultural diversity is merely a form of plural and multi-cultural *apartheid* in which each sub-culture exists only to cultivate its "own" values and protect them from contamination and domination by other value systems. The capitalist view of values implies that it is impossible for one individual, group or nation to value and learn from other value systems without its own cultural identity being threatened or watered down. Such a static, defensive view of value systems can only be challenged by a dialectical understanding of deep values as "simferences" connecting one individual, group and nation with another.

As the Jewish philosopher, Martin Buber insisted, it is the "interhuman" relationships *between* individuals within the group or community – *das Zwischenmenschliche* – that embody its true ethos. Similarly, it is the interaction *between* different social groups and classes, cultures and societies, nations and continents that is the source of cultural creativity and regeneration. From this point of view it is not the free, federal association of regions and states that threatens international cultural diversity but global capitalism. It is the latter which leads to the global domination of a single culture of marketing in which all cultural traditions and values are either sacrificed to commercial values and the pursuit of profit or turned into tourist commodities themselves. This global capitalist culture constitutes a devaluation of all deep values, replacing them with its symbolic values in the form of money, currencies, corporate logos, brand names and commercial "tittytainments".

From a socialist perspective, just as individuals can only grow by relating to each other, so cultures and value systems only grow through an interaction with *other* cultures and value systems in which each learns to value, take on board and embody elements of the other. The aim of socialism is to promote the fulfilment of all individual, group and national values, not through multicultural apartheid or the defence of the nation state but through a global trans-culture, linked to the removal of all restrictions on migration and immigration – restrictions which stand in stark contrast to the freedom of movement of international capital and of trans-national corporations. The economic objections to this ethical stand on immigration stem only from the limitations of the market economy itself. For, despite the much vaunted "globalisation" brought about by the trans-national corporations, it is the "free market" itself which, whilst allowing the free movement of goods, leads to restrictions on the free movement of people. For it creates the global inequalities of wealth which lead to barriers being set up by wealthier nations.

The very conflict between ethics and economics on questions of immigration is thus itself created by the ethics and economics of the market. The social objections to the free movement of people is based on the fear of host nations of losing their cultural or racial identity. This fear is based on the capitalist misconception that sees values and genes as private property rather than as sources of biological and cultural creativity. It also ignores the biological fact that genes themselves are activated only through the movement and migration of cells in the growing foetal body. Only in the right cellular environments are specific genes activated – through interaction with these environmental cells.

Just as biological creativity lies dormant in our genes, activated only by their migration to new environments, so does cultural creativity lie dormant in human relational potentials – in their moral genes. But the latter are also activated by the movement and migration of individuals, groups and masses and by their interaction with the social and cultural environments they find themselves in. Whether individuals or groups succeed in embodying specific qualities depends partly on the "value environment" and "value climate" of the host culture in which they are born or to which they move or migrate. Whether host and guest can value each other's qualities and acknowledge deep value kinships with each other – not only despite but *through* their symbolic value differences. For it is these differences that challenge both to truly *embody* their values in relating to each other, rather than flaunting their own cultural symbols and opposing them to each other's.

The term "moral genes" appears to express the sort of analogy drawn here between values and genes. Analogies are themselves similarities-in-difference between one process or structure and another. But the dialectical principle of simference cannot be reduced to "mere" analogy, simile or metaphor. To do so is to imply that the relation between two simferent dimensions of reality is merely a symbolic one and not also a real one. There is not merely an analogy to be drawn between values and genes, there is a real relation between them. At different stages in their lives, individuals choose to embody and express certain values rather than others, for example, in choosing between different jobs or professions, each of which draws upon different human qualities and potentials, or choosing between different geographic, social and corporate environments, each of which is pervaded with its own particular "value climate". Life decisions, big or small, always embody and/or symbolise value choices. By choosing forms of labour which call for particular human qualities, choosing environments which foster them or lifestyles which allow us to live them out, we do not merely cultivate our human potentials – we activate neurological and physiological potentials rooted in our genes. The activation and embodiment of our biological potentials, even in terms of the way our bodies look and function at different ages and stages of our lives, is not *determined* by our genes or environment, but is influenced by our value choices. Just as each of us draws from an inherited gene pool, activating those genes only in combination with other genes, so each of us draws from an inherited value pool, embodying different values and combinations of values. We do this not only by combining different life roles and juggling different elements of our lives, but by enriching each role we take in life with qualities drawn from others. This natural potential for "manipulation" of our moral genes is what is *symbolically materialised* in gene technology.

Dialogical Listening and "Communication"

Communication is a way of expressing our relationships to each other and to the material world. The same words mean different things to different people precisely because they do not have the same relationship to those things and to each other. We use language as if words had a common shared meaning, yet in order to communicate differences of meaning through them – dialogically. Speaking is not merely a mental or linguistic activity, a production of words. It is at the same time a physical, bodily activity – a vocal and gestural embodiment of the speaker's relationship to the person addressed. This *embodied meaning* may be symbolised in words, but essentially it is communicated dia-logically: through the word. It derives not from what we say but from the way we say it, who we say it to and the context in which we say it. Embodied meanings can be made explicit *in* the word, for example in writing, only in so far as language itself is, for the speaker, not a mere set of symbols but a flexible and expressive *body* of meaning.

"Body language" is not something that merely "accompanies" speech. Instead speaking *is* vocal gesturing – it *is* "body language". But nor can "verbal communication" be reduced to symbolic meaning – meanings coded in language or gestural signs. Embodied meanings are not signs: they embody the dialogical relationship of two or more speakers, their bearing towards the other. The embodied meaning of a statement is its relational meaning, the way it communicates the real relationship of the speaker to the person addressed. The *material meaning* of a statement is also a relational meaning – the way it communicates the real relationship of the speaker to the matter addressed. This, too, communicates through words, rather than in them. Material meaning only becomes fully explicit "in" language to the extent that language, spoken or written, itself takes on a material meaning or commercial value in communication – if "things" depend on language for getting them right.

The reason why the embodied and material meanings of an utterance or statement are never fully explicit in words, spoken or written, is not because language itself is an unfathomable mystery. It is because we can only put the relational, embodied or material meaning of one statement into words after it has been spoken or written, using another. Yet, this second or "metastatement" will in turn carry its own embodied and material meanings as well as linguistic and symbolic ones. This paradoxical dialectic is not an obstacle to understanding speech and language, for it is their essential dynamic – the reason why we add one more utterance or sentence to another, in the process of getting closer not just to what we are really trying to say, but to what we have said and *are saying*.

Dialogue is deep communication through the word – understood not just as the exchange of words or signs but as an active relation of individuals to each other and to the matters which they discuss. Communication in words and signs is the symbolic expression of dialogue, of the real relation of individuals to each other and the things they talk about. Dialogue and communication are therefore quite distinct. Similarly, dialogical speaking and listening are quite distinct from superficial and symbolic communicative exchanges. Deep dialogical listening allows us to hear what people are saying through their words as well as in them. But, words are not merely a symbolic expression of the relational stand people take to one another and to the things they talk about. By shaping their under-standing of things and people, they also influence their relational stand. Dialogical listening means more than just understanding what people are "really" saying through their words. It means fully understanding the words people use and what they say about them – how they shape people's relationship to each other and the world. We only really hear the *person* if we listen to their *language* as well as hearing "through" or "beneath" it. And yet, only by a listening which takes a stand under or beneath language can we do this – can we really understand someone's words as *words*, and hear the way their typical phrases and terms may be ideologically distorting or disguising their relationship to others and the world.

Deep dialogical listening generates deep thinking and questioning. It allows us to find the words to say what any given verbal exchange is really all about – the relational meanings that communicate through words. It allows us to under-stand and "think" words themselves at a deeper level, questioning the way they shape and influence people's relational stands. Above all, dialogical listening facilitates a deep speaking in which we respond to each other not just in words, but through them. For, although the *embodied meaning* of a statement can itself only be put into words after it has been uttered, that does not mean we cannot be consciously aware of this relational meaning while uttering it, nor does it mean that we should restrain ourselves from embodying it in our demeanour. To "know what I mean" is to know what my words mean to you and not just to me, to be aware, even if only in a wordless way, of the message I wish to communicate to you through these.

Words, then, are not merely a surface level of common linguistic meanings and structures, which really symbolise deeper, more personal levels of meaning, which can only be accessed through a deeper, more empathic or psychoanalytic way of listening. Nor are such deeper levels of meaning merely a reflection or construction of language itself. Deep meaning is embodied and material meaning, the communication of our real relationship to people and things. This may be unconsciously shaped by language, but speech itself need not merely reflect our existing relation to things and people – it can also establish a new one. Only dialogue is truly free speech. Only dialogical listening allows us to hear the way in which the unquestioned use of restrictive or distorting language unconsciously reproduces restricted or distorted relationships for people to each other and the world. Only deep speaking allows us to both question and challenge restrictive language in words and to respond to each other in a verbally unrestricted and fully embodied way – through our words as well as in them. This deep speaking is itself essentially a *listening speech,* for it is the way we listen to others rather than the way we respond to them in words, that both embodies our real relation to them and communicates through our words. Deep speaking is the symbolic expression of our deep *listening* relation to both language and people, word-things and worldly things.

It is the market economy which transforms things and people into symbols of their exchange value as commodities. It is the type of communicative exchange – characteristic of this economy, which transforms people's real relationships to each other and the world into a reflection of verbal jargons and ideologies. This is a type of communication that is devoid of dialogue, of dialogical listening and speaking. The less real a dialogue, the more symbolic value is attached to "communication", for what communication means in the culture of marketing is not dialogue but marketing communications. In the process of commercial exchange, the qualitative properties and use values of a commodity become the material embodiment of a common quantitative value – its exchange value, symbolised in money. In so far as communication itself takes on the character of commodity exchange, the embodied and material meaning of an utterance becomes the expression of its exchange value symbolised in words. We take each other's words literally rather than hearing through them to their embodied or material meaning. This is alright so long as the symbolic meaning of a statement – its literal meaning – is a perfect expression of its embodied and material meaning. But this is never the case. Symbolic communicative exchange always tends to shape the embodied and material meaning of statements in its own image, transforming them into the embodiment of conventional "shared meanings". In this way communication itself becomes a way of materialising shared beliefs that are embedded in conventional phraseology and terminology. Instead of communicating our relationship to each other and the world through language, language becomes a means of shaping our relationships to each other and the world ideologically – in the image of symbolic meanings and values.

To respond to something or someone "dialogically", then, is to mean something or someone through our words and not just in them. But we can only do this if we fully embody our meaning in our bodily demeanour. Only in this way do we communicate an embodied rather than purely symbolic meaning. And yet, to embody our meaning in our physical demeanour is regarded as *demeaning* in capitalist culture. Children are taught not to frown or grimace. Adults are taught to put on a cheerful mask, whatever they are feeling – particularly in serving customers or talking to their bosses. Natural demeanour is acceptable only when expressed through acceptable forms of symbolic emotional behaviour and expression. To be morose at work is unacceptable. To talk *about* one's feelings or seek counselling for "depression" is acceptable. But by the same token people are inhibited from consciously embodying their positive relational qualities in their demeanour and consciously communicating these as embodied meanings – imparting them as messages to others. Instead, all communication is supposed to be "above board" and symbolically explicit. Given this, their human qualities and feelings cease to be experienced as relational qualities. People no longer communicate their feelings through the way they relate to others – they no longer mean each other with their demeanour. Instead, their relationships with others are seen as generating feelings inside themselves or others, feelings which may have meanings but feelings which are not embodied as meanings.

Psychoanalysis and the Myth of the Talking Cure

The myth of the "talking cure" is that if emotions are not expressed or shared they can only be repressed or acted out. But feelings that are merely talked about or acted out are feelings that are not embodied.

Embodied feelings do not communicate in words but through the word: *dia-logos*. They cannot be reduced to symbolic behaviour or meanings, but are embodied in an individual's whole bearing and demeanour. The fact that someone expresses "a deep feeling of joy" or "a deep feeling of anger" does not mean that they *embody* these feelings in relating to others – in their bearing and demeanour – nor even that they have properly represented and expressed what they feel in their words and body language.

American style emotional "honesty" and "sharing" are not the expression of "deep reverence" for human feelings. Instead, they substitute the symbolic expression of deep feelings instead of actually feeling them. Feeling joy is reduced to the joy in *saying* "I feel joy"; saying "I feel angry" or "I feel sad" becomes a way of not feeling that anger or sadness deeply. In this way, the rich music of human feeling is reduced to emotions that can be labelled with words such as "joy", "anger" and "sadness". The "emotional literacy" that results is not literate at all as it restricts the wealth of human feelings to the poorest, most basic emotional lexicon. At the same time a fetish is made of "non-verbal communication" in counselling and management training where the wordless feelings embodied in an individual's bearing and demeanour are diminished to a linguistic code – an infant's ABC of gestural and postural signals whose symbolic message can be read like words and defined in words.

In this way the sharing, expression and exchange of "personal" feelings that is valued in the counter-cultures of therapy and counselling becomes everything but a communication of the *individual quality* of a person's feelings. For, this communicates only to the extent that people embody it in their bearing and demeanour, and personify it in their countenance and tone of voice. Deep feelings are not property that can be exchanged and shared. Instead it is this view of feelings as private property that generates a whole spectrum of emotional problems and conflicts. It implies that emotions are "things we feel", sometimes monstrous things that surface from the depths of the unconscious. Feelings are not things we feel – internal psychological objects. They are our way of feeling things, and of feeling other people – of touching and sensing them inwardly. They are not something we have and share but something we do.

Emotional empathy is not a process of listening and tuning into someone's feelings in order to perceive and represent them as objects. For, feelings themselves are the very *wavelengths* of attunement through which we relate to others, and on which all symbolic communication, verbal and non-verbal, rides. The qualities we embody wordlessly in our bearing and demeanour are themselves relational qualities – they embody a particular bearing towards the other person and that which they are speaking of, they embody the particular wavelength on which we tune into them. The listener does not merely tune in but sets a tone. This tone communicates to the speaker, influencing what they say and the way they say it.

Listening is not something that *precedes* our spoken response to others – that offers a dispassionate ground for insight and interpretation. The way we listen is itself a response, an embodiment of our inner bearing towards people and things – our way of feeling them. It is not "hidden" feelings but their emotional expression in words and "body language" that demand special empathic attunement on the part of the listener. For, both verbal and non-verbal communication are often a disguised or distorted symbolic expression of their own embodied and material meaning – the relational qualities that individuals embody and the embodied stand they take in relation to each other and the world. To call these relational qualities and stands "deep feelings" is one thing. To regard them *as* things and reduce them to internal objects is another.

It is not the fault of psychoanalytic theory that deep human relational qualities are objectified and turned into things. For it was Freud's genius to recognise that this objectification of feelings as word-things and word-symbols is a real process, as well as a theoretical one, in the process of dreaming. But it is the basic fault of psychoanalytic theory not to make conscious the hidden link between human relationships and communicative exchange, on the one hand, and human social relations based on private property and commodity exchange on the other. Procreative sex, and sexual relationships are not the only *embodiment* of human relational qualities. So are human creativity, labour and recreation. But in a market economy both sex and labour become commodities, reducing the individual qualities embodied in sexual and working relationships to exchangeable symbols or symbolic behaviours. The market economy and commodity exchange become the unconscious model of human communicative exchange. The culture of marketing becomes the conscious and calculated value exploitation of the human unconscious: a commercial dream factory turning unfulfilled relational qualities into *purchasable* objects, commodities.

Sexual and gender relationships have an economic dimension, just as economic and working relationships have a sexual one. Neither is driven or determined by the other, for both are an expression and embodiment of the fundamental human drive for value fulfilment. The privileging of symbolic values over "deep values" – over embodied relational qualities and kinships – is itself a distorted symbol of masculinity, and the hallmark of patriarchal cultures. In psychoanalytic theory this privileging of the Symbolic has been made into a law of human psychology.

The wordless mystery of deep human feelings lies in the fact that they can only be fully experienced and embodied relationally. Instead of seeing them as intrinsically relational qualities, however, the three major schools of psychoanalysis turn them into unconscious energies, instincts, drives or internal objects (individual or collective) which haunt relationships. This confuses human relational potentials with their distorted or disguised expression in symbolic behaviour. Relating, itself, is reduced to the projection and counter-projection, transference or counter-transference of "feelings". The psychoanalytic "relationship" aims at making the unconscious conscious in the form of words and symbols – instead of helping individuals to embody the human qualities represented by these symbols *in* their relationships.

The fourth school, that of Lacan, recognises that human relational qualities can neither be objectified in this way nor represented and interpreted by any single symbol or set of symbols. But, instead of drawing the conclusion that these qualities are meant to be embodied in relating rather than talked about, analysed or expressed in relationships, this school does quite the opposite – reducing all embodied human qualities to elusive fictions constructed by symbols, to the shadow of the Symbolic.

What the market economy achieves with the process of commercial exchange is the transformation of all material use values into commodities. What the culture of marketing achieves with the market economy is the transformation of these commodities into material symbols of valued human qualities. And what the market economy and culture of marketing have achieved in the sphere of commercial commodity exchange, Lacan's school of psychoanalysis now achieves for the process of human communicative exchange, reducing all human relationships to relationships between symbols – to language. Just as finance capitalism sees workers and factories merely as material embodiments of money, and reduces their value to symbolic values – to investment returns and share prices, so does the "science" of psychoanalysis now reduce human beings and their relationships to expressions of their word-values and communicative currencies. This is the ultimate, most refined intellectual expression of a culture in which the embodied qualities of human beings attain significance only as the embodiment of empty symbolic values, of "Signifiers" without a "signified".

Psychologising of the world...means abstraction, the attempt at a complete detachment of the soul from its basic character as relationship.   Martin Buber

The sicknesses of the soul are sicknesses of relationship. They can only be treated if I transcend the realm of the patient and add to it the world as well.   Martin Buber

Moral Education vs. Relational Learning

The term "moral education" implies that morality needs to guide education or that instruction in moral values is something that needs to be added to existing education. The basis of socialist ethics and education is the understanding that both are essentially to do with learning. Ethics is relational education: learning to value others in relationships and not merely evaluate them in one's own terms. For, to fully value others is to learn from them, and in valuing what we learn from them, to learn to value them more. Education means learning from others, not merely from teachers in the classroom but in all our relationships. What we essentially learn from another person, whether a teacher or not, comes from our relationship with that person. Good teachers do not merely pass on information and knowledge. They teach something through the way they relate to and *learn from* their students as individuals. Similarly, good partners in a relationship learn something from one another's way of being and ways of doing things. Deep relationships are educational. Deep education is relational. Deep ethics is relational education. Deep teaching is relational teaching – teaching through the way we relate to ourselves, our work and to others.

Learning from others means understanding and valuing the qualities and relational stands they embody in their way of doing things – their way of relating to themselves, each other and their work. This does not mean looking for a reflection of one's own symbolic values or ideological standpoints in others, and evaluating them on this basis, nor does it mean simply "respecting" or showing interest in theirs. It is not just a matter of identifying similarities and then putting differences to one side because "We're all the same underneath", nor of merely showing interest in such differences by becoming an "interested observer" of people's views and behaviour. Valuing others begins with appreciating their symbolic behaviour – *what* they do and say – as an embodied symbol of *who* they are, of their embodied relational qualities and stands. Valuing people in this way helps them to acknowledge the qualities they embody and materialise in their relationships, and to free themselves from distorted behaviour and beliefs they might be using to symbolise and express these. An embodied relational stand may be symbolised by an ideological "standpoint", or it may be distorted by the ideology used to

59

symbolise it. An embodied relational quality may be symbolised by a set of espoused values, but the latter may also disguise or distort the former.

"Valuing people for who they are", is, by itself, only the basis of static "co-dependent" relationships. Through it, individuals provide each other with a mutual recognition of relational qualities that their *own* words and behaviour may devalue and distort. And yet this type of valuing alone lacks spark and does not ensure a creative, dynamic relationship in which individuals learn from each other. Learning to value others in a dynamic way means valuing what we can learn from them. We do not need to share a person's religious symbols, agree with their words or accept their actions and behaviour in order to value them as people. For we know that a person's symbolic behaviour and beliefs may be a disguised and distorted expression of their relational stand and qualities – the embodied and material meaning of what they say and do. But nor do we need to accept their symbolic behaviour and beliefs as a perfect expression of these qualities in order to find something of value to us in it – to see it as a reflection, not of our own symbolic values but of human qualities *we have not yet learned to fully embody or express ourselves*. The qualities of others which we give the highest *symbolic* value to, are often those that we either undervalue or overvalue in ourselves, and therefore do not fully embody or express in our behaviour. If we symbolically undervalue a quality, we neither cherish and cultivate it, nor do we seek to embody it. It remains a potential quality only. Qualities that are symbolically undervalued or overvalued, under-represented or over-represented in our personal value politics tend to be expressed in a disguised or distorted form. If we undervalue compassion or empathy, for example, our potential for embodying these qualities might be symbolically expressed through an exaggerated capacity for self-pity. Conversely an overvalued quality of aggressive vitality might be symbolised by arrogance, brutal competitiveness or narcissism. Individuals often rely on others to represent, express or act out qualities they undervalue in themselves in an exaggerated symbolic way. If others overvalue a quality we undervalue, yet give it an exaggerated and distorted symbolic expression in their words and behaviour, this seems to justify our continuing to undervalue it.

The symbolic evaluation of human qualities in words shapes their symbolic expression in behaviour. If we symbolically associate aggression with cruel violence, for example, rather than seeing it as an embodiment of inner vitality, we will avoid all expressions of our own vitality that could be interpreted (in our own symbolic terms) as "aggressive behaviour". We will also misjudge all natural embodiments of aggressive vitality in others as "aggressiveness" and associate them with potential violence. As a result, we may dam up our natural aggressive vitality so much that it *does* indeed explode in rages, tempers or violence – our own or other's. We may, for example, attract people to us who seem to provoke such rages in us. Alternatively, we may attract people who are provoked to rage by us – thus acting out and confirming for us our own negative valuation of aggressive vitality.

All individuals attract people to themselves who embody or symbolise human *qualities* that they have not fully embodied or found ways to symbolise themselves. This is the fundamental principle of *e-quality* and mutual learning underlying all relationship and all relational learning. It applies also to therapists and counsellors as individuals, and yet the "psychodynamic" theories on which much psychotherapy and counselling is based run contrary to the equality principle of a *value-dynamic* psychology. Emotional and relational problems are regarded principally as the private property of the client, rather than as an expression of questions and issues affecting both the therapist and client. Therapists treat any echo they find of their "private" problems in the therapeutic relationship as a product of counter-transference rather than simference. "Valuing" clients is reduced to respecting, earning from, or finding professional interest and satisfaction in the therapeutic relationship. "Learning" from the therapeutic relationship begins to mean only professional and not personal learning.

Part 3

Principles and Praxis
of
Socialist Political Education

Dialectical Thinking and Dialogical Ethics

"The philosophers have only interpreted the world. The point, however, is to change it."

Karl Marx

Relational Learning and Dialogical Ethics

What is called "inter-personal communication" has to do with the market-style exchange of symbolic meanings and values expressed in communication. In communicative exchange, the parties may share a certain language and behavioural code and seek a reflection of this in the other. Alternatively they may seek to "sell" each other their own personal behaviours and beliefs, moral codes and ideologies. For, whilst these are held as private property, they are precisely for this reason also marketable and exchangeable for others. Interpersonal communication is the domain of cultural symbolism and symbolic behaviour, the ownership and exchange of symbolic meanings and values. It is also the arena of buying and selling, persuasion and resistance, conflict and negotiation, dispute and settlement. Listening in this domain is not deep dialogical listening. Instead, the listener's principal concern is whether to agree or disagree, affirm or reject, validate or invalidate another person's words – whether to "buy" them.

Beneath the plane of "interpersonal" communicative exchange lies the deeper dimension of the "inter human" – the silently sensed kinship or simference of individual human qualities that link people in relationships. It is on this level that individuals establish that intimate, wordless intercourse with one another that is embodied in sexual relations and procreation. But it is precisely because these deeply embodied value kinships ultimately defy words, that they also communicate so deeply *through* words.

The third most important dimension of the inter human is the dynamic, dialectical and dialogical relation *between* the plane of interpersonal communication and symbolic values and the deeper, more intimate, plane of inter human kinships. This dialogical dimension is the sphere of relational qualities and stands, embodied and material meanings, *both* as they are symbolised in words and symbolic behaviour and as they are communicated through these. This dialogical relation between the interpersonal and inter human sphere has two aspects. One aspect is the way in which the words and outward behaviour of one individual or group serve as the symbolic reflection of relational qualities not yet fully valued by the other – and therefore not fully embodied and fulfilled *as* values by the other. Secondly, there is the way in which one individual or group embodies relational qualities which others either symbolically reject or which they accept in a merely symbolic way (espousing them but not embodying them, accepting them only intellectually or passively complying with them behaviourally).

Interhuman and interpersonal relations are only fulfilled in relationships in which both these processes are acknowledged in dialogue ie: when individuals and groups (a) value and learn from each other's embodied qualities rather than rejecting them because of the terms in which they are expressed, and (b) value other people's "terms" themselves – each other's behaviour and beliefs – as an expression of their qualities, rather than accepting them "on their own terms".

This reciprocal valuing and learning is of course rare. More often dialogue degenerates into competition and conflict. Where reciprocal valuing and learning comes about, it is only, paradoxically, because one party takes *unilateral* responsibility for achieving it – by not pitting its own symbolic values against those of the other but by following a Dialogical Ethic. Dialogical Ethics is embodied relational learning and teaching. As such, it is not a set of values imposed upon dialogue. It is an ethic based on the intrinsic value of dialogue which seeks to fulfil this value in dialogue, through deep dialogical listening and speaking.

Deep Listening

Deep listening means not only hearing through other people's words and seeing through their behavioural signs – valuing them for who they are underneath. It means valuing their words and behaviour themselves as the symbolic expression (however distorted) of embodied and material meanings – relational standpoints and qualities – that *we* have not yet learned to fully express or embody ourselves. Only then can we begin to embody and symbolise these qualities in our own way, freeing them of distortions.

Deep Speaking

Deep speaking means consciously embodying our own relational qualities and standpoints in our bodily demeanour and letting these communicate through our words as well as in them. In particular, it means consciously embodying qualities and relational standpoints that others devalue, undervalue or value only symbolically. The best way to help another person to embody qualities they undervalue in themselves, or to take stands they find difficult to embody, is not to argue for them in words or to impose them as behaviour but to model them ourselves in the way we relate to others.

These two principles of dialogical ethics are themselves linked by a third. This third principle expresses the essential dynamic governing all human relationships. This law is not an ethical commandment but a dialectical process, the essential dynamic principle of relational learning. In any relationship between two individuals or groups, if one individual or group is able to really value the other and learn from them, then the other individual or group will find itself impelled to do the same. If it does not, then the relationship itself will dissolve or become a purely superficial and symbolic one. This principle is symbolised in a disguised and distorted way by the religious concept of "karma". Understood in terms of value dynamics, each individual or group will invariably attract friends or enemies who, by their difference-in-similarity or similarity in difference, embody and express "simferential" qualities that it has failed to embody and express itself and *for whom* it also expresses such unacknowledged simferential qualities. Opposing political and religious groups not only compete on the market place of symbolic values, they also embody, express or act out each other's deep values. Like individuals in a personal relationship, even if they do not speak or listen *to* each other, they speak for each other. They bear a message in the particular way they act or speak. To truly relate is to re-late (*relatio*) – to bear back the hidden message that is borne towards us *dia-logos* – through the word. This only happens if we first receive and heed it, value and learn from it.

The inter-personal dynamics of market-style communicative exchange is based on the *symbolic* interpretation and evaluation of other people's relational qualities, their embodied stand towards other people and things. Symbolic evaluation has only polarising results: acceptance or rejection, agreement or disagreement, curiosity or indifference. Dialogical Ethics and relational learning reverse this principle. They involve not merely valuing people for their embodied qualities but *finding value* in their symbols and behaviour themselves, however different from our own, and without needing to accept *or* reject them. This means first admitting that the political, economic or moral standpoint taken by an individual or group may not be a true expression of the embodied stand they take, or seek to take, in their relationships. That their words and actions may not truly express the embodied and material meaning of what they say and do, the actual way they relate to people and issues. The latter may be distorted and disguised by the former, but there is a fundamental distinction between them. This is a challenge to the symbolic polarisation of conflicting political standpoints that takes place in capitalist democracy – the principle that "If we are right, you are wrong." Put in other terms this means "If what we say and do is right then there is nothing of value in what you do or say." Dialogical value dynamics of relational learning and teaching challenge these two core beliefs governing human relations in capitalist society.

One belief is "If you don't do what I do, you're doing it wrong." The emotional message here is "If you don't do what I do, you're not valuing me and my way of doing." People want to be valued for who they are and the individual *way* they do things, but they confuse this with its behavioural symbol – with *what* they are (their symbolic status) and *what* they do (their symbolic behaviour). Instead of valuing their own way of doing things and embodying it more fully in their relationships, they use relationships as a way of gaining symbolic recognition for *what* they are and *what* they do.

The second core belief is "If I do what you do, I won't be able to do things my way." The emotional message here is "I fear that if I do what you do, I will lose my way and no longer be who I am." People feel that the only way they can value who they are and "be themselves" is to value what they believe they are, and what they do as a result of these beliefs. They are "stuck in their ways" without really valuing what is unique about their way of doing things.

The song of capitalist culture is "I did it my way." But why does this song need to be sung? We *cannot* do what others do without at the same time doing it our way, imbuing it with our own individual qualities. To learn from what other people do and how they do it thus presents us with no threat of losing our own way of doing things. And yet the moral conflict in capitalist society between "Doing your own thing" and doing what others do remains, hindering relational learning through the two core beliefs on which it rests.

Socialist Political Education and Organisation

Radical socialist politics cannot be a purely symbolic politics – flaunting the ethical values of "equality", "democracy" and "multiculturalism" without challenging the basic economic principles of the market. It cannot merely be a talking shop for the concerned intelligentsia or chattering classes, who fear the deep social costs accruing to this economy. Nor can its aim simply be the symbolic reshaping of democratic institutions and economic policies to give the market economy a social or democratic veneer. The deep political transformation of economic relations and the deconstruction of the market economy, nationally and internationally, can only come about on the basis of an educational transformation of the human relations which the market economy symbolises, and which it in turn reproduces. Precisely because of this, however, Deep Socialism is not an organisation of people but an organisation of ideas. Its object is not to oppose a socialist "ought" to market realities but to show the real ethical and economic contradictions inherent in the market economy – contradictions which create inherent impulses for change. It is the deep understanding of what it is that allows individuals to shed the beliefs that stand in the way of these impulses.

"The Communists do not form a separate party opposed to other working class parties" (Communist Manifesto, 1848). Deep Socialists are individuals committed to changing their human and economic relations with others, not to establishing sectarian political parties opposed to others. The means and end of Deep Socialist political praxis is socialist political education. This does not mean agitation and propaganda alone – let alone the political marketing of socialist "values". Socialist political education must be deep education as well as symbolic education, "emotional" as well as "intellectual" education, cultivating embodied knowledge as well as symbolic knowledge. But, if it is not to degenerate into a cult or sub-culture worshipping its "own" values as symbols and opposing them to those of others, socialist political education can only mean relational education, symbolic and deep. It is not only what socialists do or say, but their commitment to embodying the principles of relational learning and teaching in their personal and working lives, in the workplace, the community and the home. The embodied praxis of relational learning and therefore the embodied principle of socialist political education is Dialogical Ethics. But relational learning and teaching go together with a type of thinking which is essentially relational. The theoretical praxis of relational learning, and therefore the symbolic principle of socialist political education is Dialectical Thinking.

Dialogical Ethics is symbolised by the dialectical principle of similarity-in-difference or "simference" – that it is in their differences that individuals, groups and cultures reveal their most fundamental similarities and deep value kinships. It is the embodied understanding and application of this intellectual principle to all our human and emotional relationships – not in words, but through the word: *dia-logos*. Dialectical Thinking is the symbolic expression and intellectual application of the simference principle to our understanding of the relationship between different areas of natural and social science. Its aim is the development of a "human science of nature" and a "natural science of man".

Undialogical ethics always attempts to reduce the principle of simference to similarity or difference between individuals, groups and cultures, or else to dismiss it as an unfathomable mystery of human relations that can only be expressed through ethnic, racial or religious symbolism.

Undialectical thinking also evades or mystifies the principle of simference, reducing it to mere "simile", "analogy", or "metaphor". It ignores the real natural and social relationships between simferent processes and structures and reduces these to purely symbolic relations.

Education involves teaching and learning. The principle of socialist educational politics and socialist political education is relational learning and relational teaching. Both Dialogical Ethics and Dialectical Thinking need to be taught relationally. Teaching

Dialogical Ethics and Dialectical Thinking *relationally* means teaching others through the way we relate to them, and in this way imparting embodied knowledge and embodied human qualities. It cannot be reduced to imparting information and ideas, symbolic knowledge and symbolic values. But teaching and learning are themselves dialectically and dialogically related. To teach relationally is only possible if we can learn relationally. To teach through the way we relate to others is only possible if we can learn from the human qualities they embody in relating to us.

Teaching and learning are not symmetrical processes. Capitalist political and social education emphasises speaking and teaching, lecturing and explaining, representing and applying. Socialist political and social education must emphasise listening and learning, heeding and hearkening, taking to heart and embodying. Group culture in capitalist society takes two forms: the "workshop" in which people do things together or the "talking shop" in which they discuss things together. These are combined in closed group "meetings" with predetermined agendas of all sorts, in which people do everything but really meet as individuals. I believe a socialist group culture is based on only one essential form – the Listening Circle. This is not an "in-group" but a circle open to all, irrespective of race and religion, job and position, social, educational and ethnic background. A circle in which it is not people's symbolic values and knowledge that count most but their embodied qualities and embodied knowledge. The meeting of a Listening Circle is not a meeting with a prescribed agenda but a meeting whose sole agenda is that the participants really meet – that they explore their simferences and engage in mutual relational learning. Only out of real meeting and learning come words and actions that really mean something.

In a Listening Circle, each individual will have opportunities to speak at length, for short periods, or not at all. But all have the opportunity to listen and respond to each other. Socialist economic and cultural organisations can only emerge organically, on the basis of a free association of individuals who seek to explore and embody their deep value kinships in dialogues tuned by deep listening. Capitalist group culture brings people together in organisations and meetings solely on the basis of shared symbolic values, shared employment and professional responsibilities, shared occupations and interests, shared family or community circles. Listening Circles, on the other hand, can be convened by groups of workers and/or managers from the same company or department, or from different companies – not least *competing* companies. To these listening circles can come not only company employees but friends, partners and interested family members. Meetings of listening circles would not be social gatherings but real social *meetings* – educational meetings guided by the principles of socialist political education. No Listening Circle, whether convened by groups of employees, or by families and friends, would be closed to participants from outside the original circle – to people from other backgrounds and other communities, people in other jobs and other companies. The purpose of Listening Circles is precisely to cut across all social and economic divisions created by the market economy, whether professional and vocational, political and economic, class and cultural, national and racial. If managers and workers from related or competing companies, for example, meet without prescribed or pressured agendas to discuss the issues they confront in their working and personal lives, bringing concerned partners and interested friends along with them, then the dialogues that unfold can not only provide each individual with deep value recognition and social support, but subvert and undermine the ideologies and practices of competitive economic survival that dominate corporate culture and personal life – sowing the seeds for new forms of industrial democracy and economic management.

I do not teach. I conduct a dialogue.   Martin Buber

Socialist political leadership is not merely leadership that represents deep values and symbolises them in word and deed. It is both symbolic leadership and embodied leadership, the capacity to both represent and apply, symbolise and embody, the principles of Deep Socialism and the praxis of socialist political education. Above all, it is the capacity to initiate and conduct a dialogue. Every committed socialist can exercise political initiative and leadership by organising and convening Listening Circles – consisting initially of colleagues, friends or relatives but open to whoever wishes to participate. The art of political leadership then consists in conducting a dialogue in a way which encourages deep listening, deep speaking and deep dialectical thinking. Deep dialogue takes more time than mere communicative exchange. Deep thinking takes more time than superficial, hasty thinking.

Deep speaking takes more time than empty, hasty words. Deep listening takes more time than shallow, hasty listening. But deep listening also generates deep speaking, deep dialogue and deep dialectical thinking. It is what grants qualitative depth to the time we give to ourselves and others, deepening and enriching time itself. It is the willingness to give this quality time, and encourage others to do the same, that undermines the market economy at its roots – the belief that time is essentially *money*. Time is not saved by treating it as a "scarce resource" but by valuing its quality – by cherishing it. This is the deep thinking behind socialist ethics, economics and culture. This is the deep challenge of socialist political leadership and education.

Deep Socialism: A Manifesto of Aims

1) A progressive elimination of all pay differentials, except those based on quality of work, on the basis that no person's chosen form of labour is worth more than another's. This is not the "politics of envy" but the economics of respect for the worth of each person's labour and the deep values it embodies.

2) A progressive elimination of money and its replacement by labour quality-time-credits.

3) A progressive elimination of shareholdings, dividends and financial speculation.

4) A progressive elimination of "growth for growth's" and "profit for profit's" sake as aims of national and corporate economic planning, and its substitution with qualitative growth and deep profit maximisation – value fulfilment.

5) The progressive elimination of all environmentally damaging products and industries, and all military industries, products and "services".

6) The progressive elimination of all marketing which cheapens deep human values by transforming them into commodities.

7) A progressive introduction of local, national and international economic planning with the aim of transforming the market economy into a money-less socialist economy based on equality of labour.

8) A progressive introduction or reintroduction of free health care, of free nursery, primary, secondary and tertiary education, and free vocational training.

9) A progressive introduction of deep industrial democracy, and a culture of cooperation and relational learning in corporate life.

10) The development of new forms of health care which do not just provide profits for the health industry but instead acknowledge the symbolic and socio-somatic dimensions of health problems.

11) The promotion of the basic understanding that values and moral qualities are not the private property or monopoly of any individual, group, race, culture or religion, and that it is only by valuing other cultures and by learning from them that our own deep values are fulfilled.

12) The development of new forms of education, designed not just to provide the "labour market" with skills and abstract knowledge but to cultivate the deep embodied knowledge of both children and adults to promote relational learning – learning to value others and valuing what we learn from others.

Postscript: Capitalism, Counselling and Class

Through counselling and management consultancy, human relations workshops and management training seminars, through group dynamic therapy and psychodynamic therapy, religious communities and New Age philosophies the market economy seeks to provide, as a purchasable commodity, a marketable alternative to dialogical ethics, relational learning and the Listening Circle. In doing so, however, it transforms the relationship between trainer and trainee, counsellor and client, consultant and company, facilitator and group into a symbolic reflection of the commodity exchange process and capitalist institutional structures.

Firstly, these groups are not open and free groups. The relational learning that is cultivated begins and ends as the private property of particular "in-groups", the providers and customers. Secondly, they have their own in-built and predetermined agendas. Relational learning is itself reduced to a set of "skills" and symbolic behaviours. But training people to skilfully employ pat phrases and body signals, or to paraphrase words to make another person *feel* that they are being listened to is no substitute for really hearing them and taking these words to heart. Thirdly, training institutions for counsellors and therapists create whole hierarchies of trainees, beginners and advanced practitioners, trainers, supervisors, and supervisor trainers. These hierarchies tower above the lowly "client" at the bottom of the pyramid. They serve essentially to "filter up", contain, and keep in control the relational problems and conflicts confronting individuals and groups in society. They are designed to reflect back and ameliorate these problems symbolically through talking cures – not to tackle them at their roots. Social workers, teachers or counsellors at the social and emotional "chalk face" of this market-deformed "relational education" often end up as the victims of their case loads and as clients themselves. The filtering up of negative value from the culture of marketing, like the filtering down of positive value from the market economy, is thereby kept to a minimum.

But whatever happened to class and classes? Have the relational divisions of society into counsellor and client, religious and ethnic divisions, or the technological division of society into the "information rich" and the "information poor" replaced the division of classes? Not at all. The basic economic class division and inequality between what Marx called "proletarians" (those who live by selling their labour power) and the "bourgeoisie" (owners or shareholders of productive capital) remain. The classes have not "merged", merely overlapped. Many who own huge shareholdings are at the same time over-paid managerial employees. Yet few ordinary employees own anything more than tiny shareholdings. And nor are those non-employed shareholders and non-executive directors living off the labour of others counted amongst the unemployed. The pensions funds, which count among the major corporate shareholders are euphemistically seen as institutional investors "serving the people", like Mao's red guards. Yet investment fund managers in America themselves own shares whose total value amounts to between 10 and 15% of the entire US equity market. As for corporate managers, though they are salaried employees themselves, they become owners of capital through share option schemes and bonuses. With the increasing pressure from trans-national financial markets to increase return on capital in the name of "shareholder value" they are bought off on the side of the bourgeoisie. Class struggle does persist on both a national and international level. This is expressed not only in the battle of workers and unions to defend their jobs and pay, but in the everyday struggle of millions of individuals against value exploitation, economic and ethical, material and spiritual. The class struggle itself emerges from each individual's struggle, not only for economic survival but for deep value fulfilment.

There is indeed a fluid, classless division of society *as well as* a class one. The nature of this division was first surmised by Viktor Frankl, a psychologist and counsellor whose world outlook was forged by his experiences in the concentration camps during the Second World War. He described two axes of human life and experience central to all individuals, irrespective of class. One axis is the objective, social axis whose coordinates are "success" and "failure". The other is the subjective axis of personal experience, which moves between the twin poles of "meaning", on the one hand, and meaning-loss or despair on the other. There are individuals for whom success is combined with meaning or with meaning loss. There are individuals for whom failure is combined with either of these. Different aspects of each individual's life oscillate and move in different ways between these four coordinates.

There may indeed be meaning to be found in failure as well as success. But Frankl does not distinguish between finding "meaning" in life, which has above all to do with learning, and true value fulfilment – the satisfaction of embodying and materialising our human qualities, irrespective of whether we achieve social recognition and status – *symbolic* success. Nor does he distinguish between purely symbolic "failure" on the one hand (lack of social recognition and status) and *negative* value fulfilment – embodied in disease and war, and materialised in poverty and crime. Marxian dialectical value theory offers a different version of Frankl's two axes: the Matrix of Value Fulfilment.

One axis of the Matrix is the axis of symbolic value fulfilment – of "success" in ordinary terms. What takes us towards symbolic value fulfilment is social struggle and competition, played according to the rules of the market economy and the culture of marketing. It divides the market's "winners" and "losers". Though individuals from all classes may struggle on this axis, the struggle for symbolic recognition, status and success is, of course, inextricably bound up with class divisions and the individual's economic and class position. The other axis is that of deep rather than symbolic value fulfilment. At its negative pole are the individual and social expressions of a lack of this deep value fulfilment with embodiments of negative value such as ill-health, crime, violence and war. The movement along this axis is not one of social struggle and competition but one of individual learning and mutual cooperation. In this sense it transcends the market economy and its class divisions, for it has as its positive pole not social success but creative and relational fulfilment, growth and maturation.

The market economy rewards individuals with symbolic value fulfilment in the form of social status and power, money and symbolic commodities. In the culture of cut-throat competition, purely quantitative economic values such as "profit" and "shareholder value" compete with symbolic "moral" values such as "respect" and "trust". But all individuals remain united in the search for deep individual value fulfilment. The division and unity of individuals in society is therefore based on the different combinations of deep and symbolic value fulfilment that they experience in their lives. The Matrix of Value Fulfilment allows each of us to understand our lives – where we are and where we wish to go – in this deep, socialist way.

Each of the four quarters of the Matrix represents a different combination of symbolic and deep value fulfilment, expressed in terms of *achievement*. Both an individual's life as a whole and each sphere of their life can be seen in terms of the four categories of achievement shown on the diagram. The Matrix can thus be used to understand the nature and degree of our life achievement in each specific sphere of our lives, in terms, not merely of social success alone but of deep value fulfilment. It can help individuals to understand their life-direction too, including changes of direction towards the different poles and quarters of the Matrix. These mark out not only the essential *telos* of our lives but its real and dynamic *ethos* – for they are the product not only of social circumstance and personal drive but of free individual and ethical choice.

The Matrix of Value Fulfilment

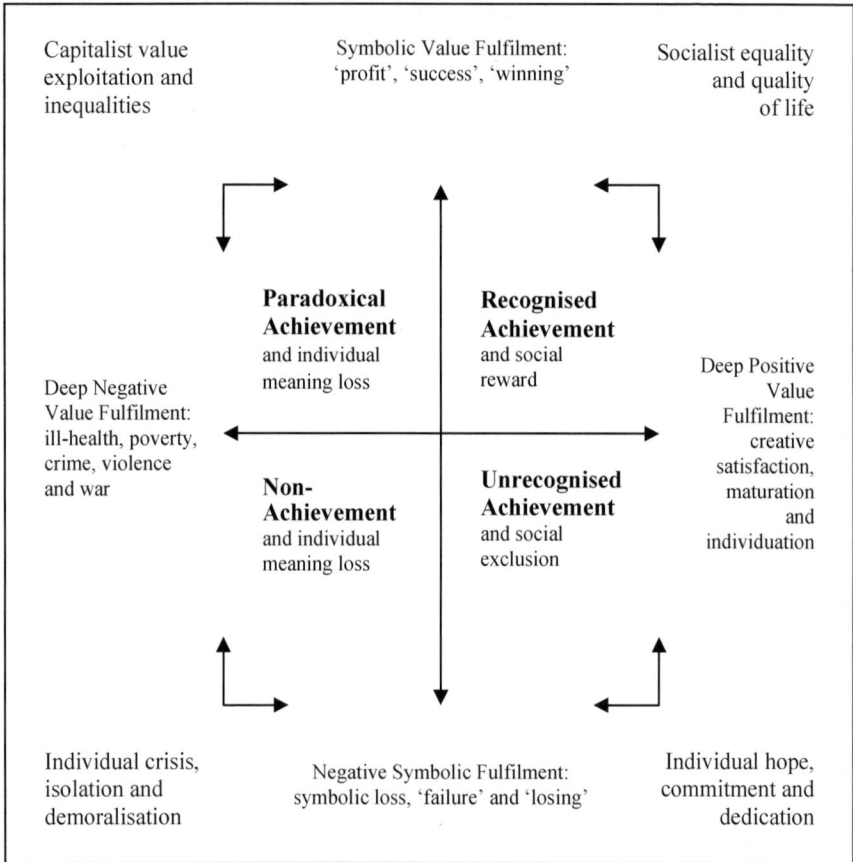

Capitalist value exploitation and inequalities

Symbolic Value Fulfilment: 'profit', 'success', 'winning'

Socialist equality and quality of life

Paradoxical Achievement and individual meaning loss

Recognised Achievement and social reward

Deep Negative Value Fulfilment: ill-health, poverty, crime, violence and war

Deep Positive Value Fulfilment: creative satisfaction, maturation and individuation

Non-Achievement and individual meaning loss

Unrecognised Achievement and social exclusion

Individual crisis, isolation and demoralisation

Negative Symbolic Fulfilment: symbolic loss, 'failure' and 'losing'

Individual hope, commitment and dedication

Bibliography

Buber, Martin *On Intersubjectivity and Cultural Creativity* Chicago 1992

Brennan, Teresa *History after Lacan* Routledge 1993

Cockshott & Cottrel *Towards a New Socialism* Spokesman 1995

Hans-Peter Martin & Harald Schumann *Die Globalisierungsfalle* Rowohlt 1997

Marx, Karl *The Communist Manifesto* 1848

Marx, Karl *Capital. A Critical Analysis of Capitalist Production*

Moore, Michael *Downsize this!* Boxtree 1997

Roberts, Jane *Dreams, Evolution and Value Fulfilment* New World Library

Roberts, Jane *The Individual and the Nature of Mass Events* NWL

Roberts, Jane *The Nature of the Psyche* NWL

The Dialectics of Value(s) –
a concise summary

The aim of socialism is deep value fulfilment, a society in which "the free development of each is the condition for the free development of all". The association of market capitalism with individualism is fundamentally false, for capitalism thrives only on proving symbolic value fulfilment.

In a market economy work itself is principally a means of symbolic value fulfilment through status, money, and the power to purchase symbolic commodities. In a socialist economy work is essentially a means of deep value fulfilment through embodiment of individual qualities in work, recreation and relationships.

The capitalist market economy is sustained and reinforced by the culture of marketing. Marketing and advertising are the "commodification" and "symbolisation" of deep values, transforming and translating deep values into marketable symbolic values.

Marketing translates deep values into symbolic ones, thus making them into commodities. Advertising and promotion use symbols to attach deep values to commodities, thus transforming them into purely symbolic values.

In the culture of marketing, individuals must also market themselves – translating and transforming their qualities into marketable words and behaviour, turning their deep values into symbolic ones and selling them as commodities.

Individuals sell the value of their labour power – the qualities they can embody and materialise in their work – only by transforming and translating them into marketable symbolic values.

The relation between individual human qualities or "deep values" and their surface or symbolic expression parallels the relation between the intrinsic value of a product – a work of art for example – and its "market value" as a commodity.

When a work of art is valued as a commodity, its sensual qualities become merely the material embodiment of its symbolic value. This symbolic value includes its value as a cultural symbol and its monetary value.

When an individual sells their labour power as a commodity, the individual qualities they embody and materialise in their work become merely the material embodiment of their symbolic value, cultural and economic.

Types of work which are culturally undervalued are also underpaid. The symbolic valuation of different types of work is a cultural valuation of the type of human qualities embodied in them.

The basis of market "demand" and market "value" is symbolic value and culturally determined symbolic valuation.

The market economy, with its differentials of pay and status, symbolises a culture of inter human relations in which individuals regard their own values as private or group property.

Instead of seeing the qualities of others as a symbolic reflection of similar-but-different qualities in themselves, people treat them as the property of others.

Instead of seeking to embody and materialise these qualities themselves, they devalue them – symbolically exalting or diminishing them, overvaluing or undervaluing them.

The only way then for them to re-appropriate these qualities is to purchase and "own" them as symbolic values – to buy them as commodities or to "buy" them as high-sounding words.

Consumption is not only material consumption but symbolic consumption – the symbolic purchase and symbolic use of values in the form of words or commodities.

The use-value of a commodity is dependent not only on its real qualities and use, but on its symbolic qualities and symbolic use.

The use-value of a word is dependent not only on its linguistic meaning and use but on its symbolic meaning and symbolic use.

The use-value of a symbol is its value in commercial or communicative exchange.

Words are both real and symbolic use-values exchanged in communication.

Commodities are both real and symbolic use-values exchanged in commerce.

Money is the universal medium of commercial exchange. Language is the universal medium of communicative exchange. Currencies are the languages of commercial exchange. Languages are the currencies of communicative exchange.

Commercial exchange transforms the real qualities and uses of a product into the outward expression of their symbolic value and symbolic use. The symbolic value of a commodity includes both its monetary value and its use as a communicative symbol – a means of communication.

Communicative exchange, dominated by the culture of marketing, transforms the linguistic meaning and use of words into the outward expression of their symbolic meaning and symbolic use.

The symbolic meaning of a word includes both its linguistic meaning and its use as a commercial symbol – a means of marketing or "selling oneself" for money.

In the culture of marketing, speaking is reduced to a form of selling, and dialogue to a negotiated communicative exchange of words and commodities – to haggling.

In the culture of marketing "listening" is reduced to symbolically valuing other people's words. "Thinking" is reduced to evaluating whether to agree or disagree with them, "buy" or not "buy" them, "invest in" or "not invest in" them.

The basis of socialist economics is the decommodification of commercial exchange – the abolition of private ownership of the means of production and labour "market", and with this the replacement of money by time-and-quality credits for labour.

The basis of socialist culture is not the devaluation of ethics, values and individual human qualities but the decommodification of individual human qualities and the deep values they embody. This requires not just the decommodification of production and distribution but the decommodification of communication.

The aim of socialist culture is the deconstruction of all shallow forms of communicative exchange dominated by symbolic values and the hollow culture of marketing, and their transformation into deep forms of dialogue.

Capitalist culture is the culture of MarCom: "Marketing Communications". Socialist culture is the culture of Deep Dialogue – through which individuals learn from each other's qualities and discover their deep value kinships.

Deep values are embodied human qualities which are communicated in the word or through the word: dia-logos; which cannot be exchanged because they are not private property in the first place but kinships or valued "simferences" connecting one individual with another.

Labour is the source of economic value creativity, because through it individual qualities are embodied and materialised.

Dialogue is the source of cultural value creativity, because it allows us to discover new value kinships with other individuals, groups and cultures, and thus to express and embody new human qualities and combinations of qualities.

Socialist economics is a labour economics, acknowledging and valuing labour as the source of economic value. Socialist ethics are dialogical ethics, acknowledging and valuing dialogue as the source of cultural value creativity.

The "values" respected in dialogical ethics are, if nothing else, the deep values of all those we engage with in dialogue. The praxis of dialogical ethics is the praxis of ethical relating in dialogue – the praxis of deepening dialogue by deepening our listening and speaking.

Deep listening is the capacity to receive another person's words as the symbolic expression (no matter how disguised or distorted) of a deep value kinship or "simference" – whether we agree or disagree with them, "buy" them or not: not to value them and evaluate them as words alone, but to hear them as an expression of particular human qualities which that person does or could embody.

Deep speaking is the capacity to respond to another person's words and behaviour, not by selling our own counter-symbols but by embodying these sensed human qualities in our own "simferent" way – thus fulfilling the kinship of deep values.

Deep thinking is the result of deep listening and the source of deep speaking.

Deep dialogue takes more time than mere communicative exchange. Deep thinking takes more time than superficial, hasty thinking. Deep speaking takes more time than empty, hasty words. Deep listening takes more time than shallow, hasty listening.

Deep listening also generates deep thinking, deep speaking and deep dialogue. It is what grants quality to the time we give to ourselves and others, deepening time itself and enriching its quality, creativity and productivity – and therefore saving time.

Time is not saved by treating it as a "scarce resource" but by valuing its quality – by cherishing it. This is the deep thinking behind socialist ethics, economics and culture.

Socialist economic and cultural organisations can only emerge organically, on the basis of a free association of individuals who seek to explore and embody their deep value kinships in dialogues tuned by deep listening.

The basic cultural form of socialist transformation is not the political party or cell but the listening circle. The listening circle is not an "in-group" but a local circle open to all, irrespective of race and religion, social, educational and ethnic background. A circle in which it is not people's symbolic values that count, but their deep ones.

Appendix: Deep Management?

Is there such a thing as radical, socialist management? Not only management for managers but management for trade unionists, staff and employees; not only business management but political and economic management, educational and health management. Management that doesn't assume a socialist economy as its starting point but anticipates and sows the seeds for one. This couldn't be a mere management style based on fashionable gurus and superficial management jargons and phraseology. It would have to be "deep management" acknowledging and taking into account deep costs as well as surface ones, deep time as well as clock time, deep values as well as symbolic ones, the deep health of its employees and their deep education as well as their "training" — the "deep ecology" of companies and communities. Management that integrates ethical and economic dimensions, making individual and collective value fulfilment its chief aim.

This means businesses that place cooperation before competition — not only with customers but with suppliers and even competitors, not only with banks but with unions and employees. Managers who provide leadership in the context of industrial democracy. Managers that can be *voted* out as well as brought in. That are expected to embody their values in their relationships as well as promote them in presentations and materialise them in quality products. Managers who know the difference between quantitative time and quality time, short-term and long-term value. Managers who do not worship the idols of profit for profit's sake and growth for growth's sake. Managers who not only respect their employees or regard them as their greatest "asset", who do not merely value them but find value in them, who can not only cultivate but learn from their qualities and grow through relating to them. Managers who are prepared to forsake their shares and bonuses, their high salaries and to be rewarded, like every other worker, on the basis of the quality of their work and not their position. Managers prepared to be humble — to receive the same basic hourly pay as all other workers. Managers able not just to act and react, to talk and negotiate, but to listen deeply.

Able not just to calculate but to meditate, not just to analyse information but to really digest it, not just to find *reasons* to justify their decisions but to cultivate their intuition — to incubate intuitive choices. Managers who meet with other managers, not just to do business but to really meet — to listen to each other in a free and open dialogue not restricted by commercial agendas. Managers who meet and engage in real human dialogue with other managers, including those of their market competitors. Managers who sow the seeds of genuine dialogue and cooperation wherever they go and whoever they meet on their business trips. Managers who have a social and political "vision" as well as a corporate one. Who listen to themselves, giving themselves time to think. Managers who understand responsibility also as deep response-ability — the capacity to respond from their core to individual and social questions. Above all, managers with the capacity to question — to dig beneath the dogmas of the market economy, and begin to dig its grave. Managers who survive and prosper not despite, but because of their values.

Also by

Peter Wilberg

The Qualia Revolution
From quantum physics to cosmic qualia science

The Madness of the Market
On the medical-psychiatric crisis of global capitalism

From Psycho-somatics to Soma-semiotics
Bodily sense and the sensed body in medicine
and psychotherapy

Heidegger, Medicine and 'Scientific Method'
The unheeded message of the Zollikon Seminars

The Therapist as Listener
Martin Heidegger and the missing dimension of psychotherapy

Head, Heart and Hara
The Soul Centres of West and East